D1055519

NOTE ON REPUBLICATION

IMMEDIATELY after midnight on Tuesday, August 23, 1927, "a good shoemaker and a poor fish peddler" were executed in the State prison at Charlestown, Massachusetts. Shortly thereafter, the letters of these two lowly men, written in self-acquired English during seven years of incarceration, were published here and in England and translated into French. Last year *The Letters of Sacco and Vanzetti* were republished in a notable paperback. Now *The Case of Sacco and Vanzetti,* originally published as a critical analysis of the record of the long drawn-out proceedings in the case up to the time of its writing in February, 1927, is being republished in the paperback of *Universal Library* wholly at its own initiation. Over the years the case has become the subject of several weighty studies and the theme of playwrights and poets. Most American historians of the period following the Great War (1914 to 1918) have found significance in the affair. And Sacco-Vanzetti have probably the unique distinction for men convicted for robbery-murder of having a favoring account of themselves in the *Dictionary of American Biography.*

In our own time there have been other, happily not many, convictions for murder which have aroused dubiety but none with such sustained concern as the executions of Sacco and Vanzetti. What accounts for this and for the sympathetic interest in the men themselves? The short and comprehensive answer was given by a group of eminent lawyers, including Newton D. Baker, Charles C. Burlingham, John W. Davis and Elihu Root, who sponsored the publication of *The Sacco-Vanzetti Case*, (Henry Holt & Company, 1928).

Since coming on the bench, I have abstained from any public comment regarding the case. This little book is a document in the history of the case. For me to deny republication would be unreasonable, for I cannot disown what I wrote thirty-four years ago. The eminent lawyers to whom I have already referred foresaw that the case "promises to be the subject of controversy and discussion for many years to come." I allow myself to say that I regard this as a sign of moral health. The reason for this belief has been stated for me by a distinguished student of historical trials. "There is no accepted test of civilization. It is not wealth, or the degree of comfort, or the average duration of life, or the increase of knowledge. All such tests would be disputed. In default of any other measure, may it not be suggested that as good a measure as any is the degree to which justice is carried out, the degree to which men are sensitive as to wrong-doing and desirous to right it?" Sir John Macdonell, *Historical Trials*, p. 148.

FELIX FRANKFURTER

Washington, D.C.
June 5, 1961

PREFATORY NOTE

THE Sacco-Vanzetti case has been before the courts and the public for more than six years. It has divided opinion at home and been the cause of demonstration abroad, and the end is not yet.

This is no ordinary case of robbery and murder. More issues are involved in it than the lives of two men. Had that been all, its history could never have been so prolonged. Other factors, little known and less understood, explain its extraordinary vitality. What they are, these pages seek to make clear, for the first time so far as the general public is concerned. There are no legal mysteries about the case which a layman cannot penetrate. The issues that are involved and the considerations relevant to their solution are within the comprehension of anyone who feels responsibility for understanding them.

F. F.

CAMBRIDGE, MASSACHUSETTS
February 15, 1927

THE CASE OF SACCO AND VANZETTI

CHAPTER I

FOR more than six years the Sacco-Vanzetti case has been before the courts of Massachusetts. Such extraordinary delay, in a state where ordinarily murder trials are promptly dispatched, in itself challenges attention. A long succession of disclosures has aroused interest far beyond the boundaries of Massachusetts and even of the United States, until the case has become one of those rare *causes célèbres* which are of international concern. My aim is to give in brief compass an accurate résumé of the facts of the case from its earliest stages to its present posture. The following account is based upon the record of the successive court proceedings through which the case has gone, with such references to extrinsic facts as are necessary for understanding what transpired in court. Obviously, to tell the story within limited space requires drastic compression. The necessary selection of material has been guided by canons of relevance and fairness familiar to every lawyer called upon to make a disinterested summary of the record of a protracted trial. The entire record, spread over many thousand pages, is accessible to anyone who desires to examine for himself the ground herein traveled.

At about three o'clock in the afternoon of April 15, 1920, Parmenter, a paymaster, and Berardelli, his

guard, were fired upon and killed by two men armed
with pistols, as they were carrying two boxes containing the pay roll of the shoe factory of Slater and Mor
rill, amounting to $15,776.51, from the company's
office building to the factory through the main street
of South Braintree, Massachusetts. As the murder
was being committed a car containing several other
men drew up to the spot. The murderers threw the
two boxes into the car, jumped in themselves, and were
driven away at high speed across some near-by railroad tracks. Two days later this car was found abandoned in woods at a distance from the scene of the
crime. Leading away from this spot were the tracks
of a smaller car. At the time of the Braintree holdup
the police were investigating a similar crime in the
neighboring town of Bridgewater. In both cases a
gang was involved. In both they made off in a car.
In both eyewitnesses believed the criminals to be
Italians. In the Bridgewater holdup the car had left
the scene in the direction of Cochesett. Chief Stewart
of Bridgewater was therefore, at the time of the
Braintree murders, on the trail of an Italian owning
or driving a car in Cochesett. He found his man in
one Boda, whose car was then in a garage awaiting
repairs. Stewart instructed the garage proprietor,
Johnson, to telephone to the police when anyone came
to fetch it. Pursuing his theory, Stewart found that
Boda had been living in Cochesett with a radical named
Coacci. Now on April 16, 1920, which was the day
after the Braintree murders, Stewart, at the instance
of the Department of Justice, then engaged in the

rounding-up of Reds, had been to the house of Coacci to see why he had failed to appear at a hearing regarding his deportation. He found Coacci packing a trunk and apparently very anxious to get back to Italy as soon as possible. At the time (April 16), Coacci's trunk and his haste to depart for Italy were not connected in Chief Stewart's mind with the Braintree affair. But when later the tracks of a smaller car were found near the murder car, he surmised that this car was Boda's. And when he discovered that Boda had once been living with Coacci, he connected Coacci's packing, his eagerness to depart, his actual departure, with the Braintree murders, and assumed that the trunk contained the booty. In the light of later discoveries Stewart jumped to the conclusion that Coacci, Boda's pal, had "skipped with the swag." As a matter of fact, the contents of the trunk, when it was intercepted by the Italian police on arrival, revealed nothing. In the meantime, however, Stewart continued to work on his theory, which centred around Boda: that whosoever called for Boda's car at Johnson's garage would be suspect of the Braintree crime. On the night of May 5, Boda and three other Italians did in fact call.[1]

To explain how they came to do so let us recall here the proceedings for the wholesale deportation of Reds under Attorney-General Palmer in the spring of 1920. In particular the case of one Salsedo must be borne in mind—a radical who was held incommunicado in a

[1] See letter of Thomas O'Connor in the *Boston Herald* for November 14, 1926.

room in the New York offices of the Department of Justice on the fourteenth floor of a Park Row building. Boda and his companions were friends of Salsedo. On May 4 they learned that Salsedo had been found dead on the sidewalk outside the Park Row building, and, already frightened by the Red raids, bestirred themselves to "hide the literature and notify the friends against the federal police." For this purpose an automobile was needed and they turned to Boda. Such were the circumstances under which the four Italians appeared on the evening of May 5 at the Johnson garage. Two of them were Sacco and Vanzetti. Mrs. Johnson telephoned the police. The car was not available and the Italians left, Sacco and Vanzetti to board a street car for Brockton, Boda and the fourth member, Orciani, on a motor cycle. Sacco and Vanzetti were arrested on the street car, Orciani was arrested the next day, and Boda was never heard of again.

Stewart at once sought to apply his theory of the commission of the two "jobs" by one gang. The theory, however, broke down. Orciani had been at work on the days of both crimes, so he was let go. Sacco, in continuous employment [1] at a shoe factory

---

[1] At the trial Sacco's employer testified as follows about him: "* * * he was a very steady worker. He worked very steady from seven in the morning until quitting time at night and was on the job every day that you could expect any healthy man to work. There was times when he was two or three hours late on account of sickness, but outside of his getting through and talking of going to the old country, he was absolutely on the job every day." (R. 460.)

[Author's Note: In the interest of convenience in the frequent references to the court proceedings the following abbreviations will be used:

in Stoughton, had taken a day off (about which more later) on April 15. Hence, while he could not be charged with the Bridgewater crime, he was charged with the Braintree murders; Vanzetti, as a fish peddler at Plymouth and his own employer, could not give the same kind of alibi for either day, and so he was held for both crimes.[1] Stewart's theory that the crime was committed by these Italian radicals was not shared by the head of the state police, who always maintained that it was the work of professionals.

Charged with the crime of murder on May 5, Sacco and Vanzetti were indicted on September 14, 1920,

---

"R." means "Defendants' Exceptions in Commonwealth of Massachusetts *vs.* Nicola Sacco and Bartolomeo Vanzetti"; "M. R." means "Defendants' Amended Bill of Exceptions on Motion for New Trial, 1926."]

[1] In an account of the joint trial of Sacco and Vanzetti the details of Vanzetti's separate trial cannot find a place, but Vanzetti's prosecution for the Bridgewater job grew out of his arrest for, and was merely a phase of, the Braintree affair. The evidence of identification of Vanzetti in the Bridgewater case bordered on the frivolous, reaching its climax in the testimony of a little newsboy who, from behind the telegraph pole to which he had run for refuge during the shooting, had caught a glimpse of the criminal and "knew by the way he ran he was a foreigner." Vanzetti was a foreigner, so of course it was Vanzetti! There were also found on Vanzetti's person, four months after the Bridgewater attempt, several shells, one of which was claimed to be of a type similar to shells found at the scene of the Bridgewater crime. The innocent possession of these shells was accounted for at the Dedham trial. More than twenty people swore to having seen Vanzetti in Plymouth on December 24, among them those who remembered buying eels from him for the Christmas Eve feasts. Of course all these witnesses were Italians. The circumstances of the trial are sufficiently revealed by the fact that Vanzetti, protesting innocence, was not allowed by his counsel to take the witness stand for fear his radical opinions would be brought out and tell against him disastrously. From a verdict of conviction counsel took no appeal. The judge and district attorney were Judge Webster Thayer and Mr. Katzmann, as also in the Braintree trial. The Bridgewater conviction was played up with the most lurid publicity when Vanzetti faced his trial for the Braintree crime.

and put on trial May 31, 1921, at Dedham, Norfolk County. The setting of the trial, in the courthouse opposite the old home of Fisher Ames, furnished a striking contrast to the background and antecedents of the prisoners. Dedham is a quiet residential suburb, inhabited by well-to-do Bostonians with a surviving element of New England small farmers. Part of the jury was specially selected by the sheriff's deputies from persons whom they deemed "representative citizens," "substantial" and "intelligent." The presiding judge was Webster Thayer of Worcester. The chief counsel for these Italians, Fred H. Moore, was a Westerner, himself a radical and a professional defender of radicals. In opinion, as well as in fact, he was an "outsider." Unfamiliar with the traditions of the Massachusetts bench, not even a member of the Massachusetts bar, the characteristics of Judge Thayer unknown to him, Moore found neither professional nor personal sympathies between himself and the Judge. So far as the relations between court and counsel seriously, even if unconsciously, affect the temper of a trial, Moore was a factor of irritation and not of appeasement. Sacco and Vanzetti spoke very broken English, and their testimony shows how often they misunderstood the questions put to them. A court interpreter was used, but his conduct raised such doubts[1] that the defendants brought their own interpreter to check his questions and answers. The trial lasted nearly seven weeks, and on July 14, 1921, Sacco and Vanzetti were found guilty of murder in the first degree.

[1] Some time after the trial this interpreter was convicted of larceny.

CHAPTER II

So far as the crime is concerned we are dealing with a conventional case of pay-roll robbery resulting in murder. At the trial the killing of Parmenter and Berardelli was undisputed. The only issue was the identity of the murderers. Were Sacco and Vanzetti two of the assailants of Parmenter and Berardelli, or were they not? This was the beginning and the end of the inquiry at the trial; this is the beginning and the end of any judgment now on the guilt or innocence of these men. Every other issue, no matter how worded, is relevant only as it helps to answer that central question.

On that issue there was at the trial a mass of conflicting evidence. Fifty-nine witnesses testified for the Commonwealth and ninety-nine for the defendants. The evidence offered by the Commonwealth was not the same against both defendants. The theory of the Commonwealth was that Sacco did the actual shooting and that Vanzetti sat in the car as one of the collaborators in a conspiracy to murder. Witnesses for the Commonwealth testified to having seen both defendants in South Braintree on the morning of April 15; they claimed to recognize Sacco as the man who shot the guard Berardelli and to have seen him subsequently escape in the car. Expert testimony (the character of which, in the light of subsequent events, constitutes one of the most important features of the case) was offered seeking to connect one of four bullets removed from Berardelli's body with the Colt pistol found on Sacco at the time of his arrest. As to Vanzetti, the Commonwealth adduced evidence placing him in the murder car. Moreover, the Commonwealth introduced the conduct of the defendants, as evinced by pistols found on their persons and lies admittedly told by them when arrested, as further proof of identification in that such conduct revealed "consciousness of guilt."

The defense met the Commonwealth's eyewitnesses by other eyewitnesses, slightly more numerous than those called by the Commonwealth and at least as well circumstanced to observe the assailants, who testified that the defendants were not the men they saw. Their testimony was confirmed by witnesses who proved the presence of Sacco and Vanzetti elsewhere at the time of the murder. Other witnesses supported Sacco's testimony that on April 15 — the day that he was away from work — he was in Boston seeing about a passport to Italy, whither he was planning shortly to return to visit his recently bereaved father. The truth of his statement was supported by an official of the Italian consulate in Boston who deposed that Sacco visited his consulate at 2.15 P.M. If this were true, it was conceded that Sacco could not have been a party to this murder. The claim of Vanzetti that on April 15 he was pursuing his customary trade as fish peddler was sustained by a number of witnesses who had been his customers that day.

From this summary it must be evident that the trustworthiness of the testimony which placed Sacco and Vanzetti in Braintree on April 15 is the foundation of the case.

I. As to Sacco: —
The character of the testimony of the five witnesses who definitely identified Sacco as in the car or on the spot at the time of the murder demands critical attention. These witnesses were Mary E. Splaine, Frances Devlin, Lola Andrews, Louis Pelzer, Carlos E. Goodridge.

1. Splaine and Devlin were working together on the second floor of the Slater and Morrill factory, with windows giving on the railroad crossing. Both heard the shot, ran to the window, and saw an automobile crossing the tracks. Splaine's identification of Sacco, as one of the occupants of this escaping car, was one of the chief reliances of the prosecution. Splaine, viewing the scene from a distance of from 60 to 80 feet, saw a man previously unknown to her, in a car traveling at the rate of from 15 to 18 miles per hour; she saw him only for a distance of about 30 feet, that is to say, for from one and a half to three seconds; and yet she testified: —

The man that appeared between the back of the front seat and the back seat was a man slightly taller than the witness. He weighed possibly from 140 to 145 pounds. He was muscular, an active looking man. His left hand was a good sized hand, a hand that denoted strength.

Q. So that the hand you said you saw where? A. The left hand, that was placed on the back of the front seat, on the back of the front seat. He had a gray, what I thought was a shirt, — had a grayish, like navy color, and the face was what we would call clear-cut, clean-cut face. Through here [indicating] was a little narrow, just a little narrow. The forehead was high. The hair was brushed back and it was between, I should think, two inches and two and one-half inches in length and had dark eyebrows, but the complexion was a white, peculiar white that looked greenish. (R. 114–5.)

Q. Is that the same man you saw at Brockton?   A. It is.

Q. Are you sure?   A. Positive. (R. 115.)

The startling acuity of Splaine's vision was in fact the product of a year's reflection. Immediately after Sacco's arrest the police, in violation of approved police methods for the identification of suspects, brought Sacco alone into Splaine's presence. (R. 121, 130.) Then followed in about three weeks the preliminary hearing at which Sacco and Vanzetti were bound over for the grand jury. At this hearing Splaine was unable to identify Sacco: —

Q. You don't feel certain enough in your position to say he is the man?   A. I don't think my opportunity afforded me the right to say he is the man. (R. 132.)

When confronted with this contradiction between her uncertainty forty days after her observation and her certainty more than a year after her observation, she first took refuge in a claim of inaccuracy in the transcript of the stenographer's minutes. This charge she later withdrew and finally maintained: —

From the observation I had of him in the Quincy court and the comparison of the man I saw in the machine, on reflection I was sure he was the same man. (R. 133.)

Then followed this cross-examination: —

Q. You now say that on reflection you feel sure he is the man? A. I feel most certain he is.

Q. You were answering in the lower court from your observation, were n't you? A. Yes, sir.

Q. From what you saw? A. Yes.

Q. Your answer now is that you feel most certain that he is? A. Yes.

Q. That is not the position that you are sure beyond any doubt, is it? You are most certain now, are n't you? A. I am positive he is the man; certain he is the man. I admit the possibility of an error, but I am certain I am not making a mistake.

Q. Your answer in the lower court was you did n't have opportunity to observe him. What did you mean when you said you did n't have opportunity sufficient, kindly tell us, you did n't have sufficient opportunity to observe him? A. Well, he was passing on the street.

Q. He was passing on the street and you did n't have sufficient opportunity to observe him to enable you to identify him? A. That is what I meant.

Q. That is the only opportunity you had? A. Yes, sir.

Q. You have had no other opportunity but that one fleeting glance? A. The remembrance of that. (R. 133.)

Let Dr. Morton Prince, professor of abnormal and dynamic psychology at Harvard University, comment on this testimony: —

I do not hesitate to say that the star witness for the government testified, honestly enough, no doubt, to what was psychologically impossible. Miss Splaine testified, though she had only seen Sacco at the time of the shooting from a distance of about 60 feet for from 1½ to three seconds in a motor car going at an increasing rate of speed at about 15 to 18 miles an hour; that she saw and at the end of a year she remembered and described

14THE CASE OF SACCO AND VANZETTI

16 different details of his person, even to the size of his hand, the length of his hair as being between two and 2½ inches long, and the shade of his eyebrows! Such perception and memory under such conditions can be easily proved to be psychologically impossible. Every psychologist knows that — so does Houdini. And what shall we think of the animus and honesty of the state that introduces such testimony to convict, knowing that the jury is too ignorant to disbelieve?

How came Miss Splaine to become acquainted with these personal characteristics of Sacco?

The answer is simple. Sacco had been shown to her on several occasions. She had had an opportunity to study him carefully. More than this, he sat before her in the court. At the preliminary hearing in the police court she was not asked to pick Sacco from among a group of other men. Sacco was shown alone to her. Every one knows that under such circumstances the image of a person later develops, or may develop, in an observer's mind and becomes a false memory. Such a memory is produced by suggestion. Every lawyer knows the unconscious falsification of memory due to later acquired knowledge, though ignorant of the psychology of the phenomenon. And yet Miss Splaine's testimony was offered by the state to the jury.

Why was not Miss Splaine asked to pick out Sacco from among a group of men? If this had been done, this unconscious falsification of memory would have been avoided.[1]

As a matter of fact "the good-sized hand" by which Splaine identified Sacco and on which, in a later affidavit, she rests her identification almost entirely, did not exist. Sacco has hands smaller than the average. (M. R. 165.) Also, since the trial it has been shown that Splaine had identified another person as the man whom she later identified as Sacco, after it appeared

[1] Letter, "A Psychologist's Study," *Boston Herald*, October 30, 1926.

that the person previously identified by her was in jail on April 15, 1920. (M. R. 180.)

2. Devlin, a little over a month after the murders, thus testified: —

He (Sacco) looks very much like the man that stood up in the back seat shooting. (R. 274.)

"Q. Do you say positively he is the man?" and you answered: "A. I don't say positively." (R. 275.)

At the trial, over a year later, she had no doubt, and when asked: "Have you at any time had any doubt of your identification of this man?" (R. 276) replied: "No." The obvious discrepancy of an identification reaching certainty by lapse of time, without any additional opportunity for verification, she explained thus: —

At the time there I had in my own mind that he was the man, but on account of the immensity of the crime and everything, I hated to say right out and out. (R. 276.)[1]

[1] The process by which casual observation of a stranger is in process of being translated into positive identification is illustrated in a recent New York case in which conviction for murder, based on tenuous identification, was reversed. In the course of his opinion the Chief Judge of the New York Court of Appeals wrote as follows: —

"Thus in a final analysis the conviction of defendant must basically rest upon the asserted similarity of his eyes to those of a man whom the witness momentarily saw looking at her through a window when she had no occasion to exercise a complete and careful scrutiny. That is a pretty small basis upon which to rest a conviction and, as we read the testimony of the witness as it proceeds from the friendly atmosphere of direct and redirect examination to the hostile one of cross-examination with its more exacting and insistent questions, it seems to us that she, acting upon a small foundation, has rather reasoned herself, conscientiously we have no doubt, into the belief that defendant is the man whom she saw at the farm and that her attempted identification is the result of a conclusion thus developed and clouded by more or less doubt and uncertainty rather than

The inherent improbability — not to say, as does Dr. Prince, "impossibility" — of making any such accurate identification on the basis of a fleeting glimpse of an unknown man in the confusion of a sudden alarm is affirmed by the testimony of two other eyewitnesses. Ferguson and Pierce, from a window above Splaine and Devlin, on the next floor of the factory, had substantially the same view as the two women. They found it impossible to make any identification.

Thus Ferguson: —

He thinks that he did testify at the inquest in response to the question "How did that man look?" as follows: — "I can't tell it [*sic*] all. I only had a quick glimpse of him. He looked like an Italian with a growth of beard. It seems just as he shot he just got up from the front seat, and it seems to me he was pulling his cap over his hair."

He did testify at the inquest in response to the question "If you saw a picture, could you recognize him?" as follows: — "I feel pretty sure I could not."

Q. And you can't recognize him now? A. No, sir. (R. 548-9.)

Then Pierce: —

Q. Would you be able to tell the men, the chauffeur, and the man in the front seat? A. I don't think so. I have had pictures shown me by the state police and if it was a matter of looking at a million pictures I could n't say. I just saw a dark man with a gun, that is all. (R. 544.)

---

an identification based upon reliable and decisive observations carried by a definite recollection to a conclusion whose correctness admits of no reasonable doubt. If this is a correct estimate of her testimony the conviction ought not to stand and the man be executed." *People* v. *Klvana*, 241 N. Y. 481, 487-8 (1926).

3. Pelzer, a young shoe-cutter, swore that when he heard the shooting he pulled up his window, took a glance at the scene, and saw the man who murdered Berardelli: —

Q. How long did you stay in the window? A. Oh, about, — I would say about a minute. * * *
Q. Then what did you do? A. I seen everything happen about that time, about in a minute. (R. 157.)

This was the foundation for the following identification: —

Q. Do you see in the court room the man you saw shooting Berardelli that day? A. Well, I would n't say it was him but he is a dead image of him.
Witness points out Mr. Sacco.
Q. Have you seen him since that time until you saw him in the court room? A. No, sir.
Witness was shown picture of him by Mr. Williams today.
Q. You say you would n't say it is him, but he is the dead image of him? What do you mean by that? A. Well, he has got the same appearance. (R. 155.)

On cross-examination Pelzer admitted that immediately after Sacco's arrest, on May 6 or 7, he was unable to make any identification: —

I did not see enough to be able to identify anybody. (R. 175.)

Pelzer's inability in May 1920 to make the identification which he did make in June 1921 was confirmed by three fellow workmen, at work in the same room on the day of the murder. Two of them testified that instead of pulling up the window he took shelter under a bench, and the third added: —

Q. Did you hear him later talk about the shooting? A. I think I did, but I am not sure.

Q. That day? A. Yes, sir. * * *

Q. What did you hear Pelser say? A. Well, I heard him say that he did not see anybody. . . . That is all.

Q. Is that all you recollect that you heard him say? A. Yes, sir. (R. 581.)

Pelzer's tergiversations and falsifications extracted from the District Attorney, Mr. Katzmann, the following eulogy: —

He was frank enough here, gentlemen, to own that he had twice falsified before to both sides, treating them equally and alike, and he gave you his reason. I think he added that he had never been in court before. If not, somebody has and I confused him. It is of little consequence. He is big enough and manly enough now to tell you of his prior falsehoods and his reasons for them. If you accept them, gentlemen, give such weight to his testimony as you say should be given. (R. 1130.)

4. Lola Andrews, a woman of doubtful reputation, testified that at about 11 A.M. on the day of the murders, while in company with a Mrs. Campbell, she saw an automobile standing outside the Slater and Morrill factory. She saw a "very light" man inside the car (concededly neither Sacco nor Vanzetti) and another man "bending over the hood of the car," whom she characterized as a "dark-complexioned man." She went into the factory in search of a job and at the time "had no talk with either of the men." When she came out "fifteen minutes later" the dark man "was down under the car like he was fixing something" and she asked him the way to another factory. He told her. That was the whole conversation between

them. After Sacco's arrest she was taken to the Dedham jail and identified Sacco as the dark-complexioned man. She again identified him at the trial.

How came she to connect the dark man under the car with the murder which took place four hours later?

Q. Would you say that the man had a fuller or more slender face [than the man in a photograph shown to the witness]? A. I don't know. He had a funny face. * * *

Q. Meaning by that a face that was not a kindly face, a kind of brutal face? A. He did not have a real good looking face. (R. 198.)

Q. [By the Commonwealth] What came to your mind, if anything, when you learned of the shooting? * * * A. Why, the only way I can answer that is this: When I heard of the shooting I somehow associated the man I saw at the car. (R. 251-2.)

Four reputable witnesses completely discredited the Andrews testimony.

A. Mrs. Campbell, an elderly woman who was with Andrews throughout the episode, testified that, while they saw an automobile in front of the factory, the man they accosted for information was not the man under the automobile but a man "in khaki clothes" standing near (R. 624): —

When they came out neither she nor Mrs. Andrews spoke to a man at the automobile in front of the Slater & Morrill factory.

Q. Did you hear Mrs. Andrews have any talk with any man who was working around an automobile that morning? A. No, sir.

Q. Did Mrs. Andrews speak to a man? A. No, sir.

Q. (continued) Who was working about an automobile that morning? A. No, sir. (R. 625.)

B. Harry Kurlansky testified as follows: —

He is in business at Quincy, at 1466 Hancock Street. He has been in business there since 1909 or 1910. He knows Mrs. Lola Andrews and has known her for the last seven or eight years. Sometime in February of this year he had a talk with her. "I was right on my door step and Lola Andrews went by . . . It was just between six or seven; I should judge it was about half past six."

Q. Now, tell us what was said. A. As I sat on my door step and as I know her I always spoke to her when she went by. I said to her, "Hello, Lola," and she stopped and she answered me. While she answered me I said, "You look kind of tired." She says, "Yes." She says, "They are bothering the life out of me." I says, "What?" She says, "I just come from jail." I says, "What have you done in jail?" She says, "The Government took me down and want me to recognize those men," she says, "and I don't know a thing about them. I have never seen them and I can't recognize them." She says, "Unfortunately I have been down there to get a job and I have seen many men that I don't know and I have never paid any attention to anyone." (R. 638–9.)

This patently ingenuous witness was subjected to the following questioning by Judge Thayer: —

THE COURT. Mr. Witness, I would like to ask you one question. Did you attempt to find out who this person was who represented the Government who was trying to get her to take and state that which was false?

THE WITNESS. Did I what?

MR. JEREMIAH MCANARNEY. What is that question?

THE COURT. Did you try to find out who it was who represented the Government?

THE WITNESS. No.

THE COURT. Why not?

THE WITNESS. Well, it did n't come into my mind. I was n't sure, you know. It did n't —

THE COURT. Did you think the public interest was served by anybody representing the Government to try to get a woman —

THE WITNESS. I don't think of anything —

THE COURT. — To identify somebody? * * *

THE WITNESS. I don't think of anything like that, just simply what she tell you.

THE COURT. Don't you think it would be a good idea to find out, if you could?

THE WITNESS. I think it would be.

THE COURT. I am trying to find out why you did n't do it. (R. 641.)

Q. (By Mr. McAnarney) Did you regard it as any of your business or any of your duty to look up and see who the Government man was who was with Mrs. Andrews? A. Why should I bother about it? (R. 640, 641.)

This cross-examination must appear strange to anyone familiar with the usual conduct of Massachusetts trial judges. For Judge Thayer to insist that it was the duty of a small shopkeeper, poorly educated and struggling with imperfect English, to ferret out intimations of police improprieties conveyed in the course of a casual conversation was to draw a "red herring" across the trail. It undoubtedly served to discredit Kurlansky in the eyes of the jury and thereby to obliterate the effect of important testimony adverse to the Commonwealth. Only the extraordinary features of this case, as they will unfold in the course of the subsequent discussion, can account for the incident.

C. In February 1921, Andrews complained to the police of an assault on herself in her apartment in

Quincy.   George W. Fay, a Quincy policeman who was called in to investigate the matter, gave the following account of his conversation with Andrews: —

I asked her if the man who assaulted her, if she thought that he was one of the men she saw at Braintree on the day of the shooting, and she said she could not tell because she did not see the faces of the Braintree men. I asked her how he compared in appearance with the men at Braintree that she saw. She said that she could not tell. I asked her if his clothes were like the clothes that any of the men wore at Braintree, she said she could not tell. (R. 637.)

D. Alfred Labrecque, a Quincy newspaper man and secretary of the Quincy Chamber of Commerce, testified to a conversation with Andrews substantially to the same effect as Fay's.

The District Attorney not only offered the Andrews testimony for the consideration of the jury, but gave it the weightiest possible personal sponsorship: —

Gentlemen, there is some responsibility upon the Commonwealth.   There is some responsibility upon a prosecutor who produces witnesses whose evidence tends to prove murder. He may think well. He should think long, and he should always have his intelligence and his conscience with him before he puts the stamp of approval of the Commonwealth of Massachusetts upon him as a credible witness before he takes the stand seeking to prove the guilt of men and if proven will result in their death. (R. 1127.)

And then there is Lola Andrews. I have been in this office, gentlemen, for now more than eleven years. I cannot recall in that too long service for the Commonwealth that ever before I have laid eye or given ear to so convincing a witness as Lola Andrews. (R. 1131.)

5. Carlos E. Goodridge (who after the trial was discovered to be a fugitive from justice in another state and to have given evidence under a false name) swore that, at the time of the shooting, he was in a poolroom in South Braintree, heard shots, stepped to the door, saw an automobile coming toward him, and when he got to the sidewalk a man in the automobile "poked a gun over towards him," whereupon he "went back into the poolroom." (R. 304.) About seven months later, he identified Sacco as that man for the first time and identified him again at the trial.

Four witnesses squarely contradicted Goodridge's belated identification.

A. Goodridge reported the affray to his employer, Andrew Manganaro, an hour afterward without revealing any identification. Manganaro further testified: —

Later at the time that Sacco and Vanzetti were arrested there was another talk between the witness and Goodridge. The witness read of the arrest in the newspapers and the same day went to the South Braintree store and told Mr. Goodridge that he should go and see if he could recognize these people that were arrested, whether they were the ones or not.

Q. What did he say? A. He said he could not do it because when he saw the gun he was so scared he run right in from where he was. He could not possibly remember the faces. I told him as a matter of justice, "if you think you do remember the faces do go over there and I will pay you just the same." (R. 647–8.)

Finally, Manganaro testified without contradiction that Goodridge's reputation for veracity was bad.

B. Magazu, who ran the poolroom in combination
with a shoe store, testified as follows: —

While I showed the customer a pair of shoes, he comes right in
and says, "My God, something wrong about down the street."
I says, "What?" He says "I think they kill the paymaster
and get the payroll." I says, "Did you see the men?" He
says, "I seen the men, they pointed with a gun." I says,
"How do the men look like?" He says "Young man with
light hair, light complexion and wore an army shirt."
Q. Which man? A. One man pointing with a gun. I don't
know which.
Q. Did he say anything further about it to you? A. He
says, "This job was n't pulled by any foreign people." (R. 632.)

C. Arrogni, a barber in South Braintree, gave the
following evidence: —

About a week or so after April 15, 1920, he had a talk with
Goodridge in the barber's shop. Goodridge said to him in the
course of this conversation: "I was in the pool-room and I
heard some shots and I looked through the window and I saw
the bandit car come up and I saw a man in the car, but if I
have got to say who the man was, I can't say." (R. 631.)

D. Arrogni's boss, Damato, swore to the same
effect.

Even when completely disinterested, identification
testimony runs all the grave hazards due to the frailties
and fallibilities of human observation and memory.
But Goodridge's testimony was, in addition to everything else, tainted with self-interest. At the time he
was a witness for the Commonwealth, he was facing
jail under an indictment for larceny to which he had
pleaded guilty. The case "had been filed," — that
is, no sentence had been imposed, — and Goodridge

had been placed on probation. The Judge did not allow the defense to show that Goodridge's testimony on behalf of the Commonwealth was influenced by leniency previously shown to him by the District Attorney in connection with the confessed charge of larceny, and by fear of losing his immunity. In the light of settled principles of the law of evidence this ruling, though later sustained by the Supreme Judicial Court of Massachusetts,[1] is indefensible.[2]

II. As to Vanzetti: —

The Commonwealth offered two witnesses who claimed to identify Vanzetti as an occupant of the murder car. Of these one, Dolbeare, claimed to have seen him hours before the murder, leaving only a single individual, LeVangie, who claimed to have seen him on the spot. Before dealing with Dolbeare and LeVangie, a few words will dispose of two other witnesses who claimed to have seen Vanzetti during the day of the murder elsewhere than at Plymouth, but not at South Braintree. One witness, Faulkner, testified to recollecting a fellow passenger on a train going from Cochesett to Boston who got out at East Braintree at 9.54, and identified Vanzetti as that passenger. The basis of Faulkner's recollection was so frail and was so fully destroyed by three other witnesses (McNaught, Pratt, and Brooks), all railroad men, that

---

[1] 151 N. E. 839, 851; 255 Mass. 369.

[2] This opinion is ventured on the authority of three members of the Harvard Law School faculty especially versed in the law of evidence. Of course, it is not urged that, had this been the only error of Judge Thayer, it would have justified the granting of a new trial. For a technical criticism of this ruling see 36 Yale Law Journal 384, 388.

we deem it superfluous to make a further recital of
his testimony. Finally Reed, a crossing tender, pur-
ported to recognize Vanzetti as the man sitting on
the front seat of a car which he claimed to identify
as the murder car. This was at some distance more
than an hour after the murder. Reed's testimony
placing Vanzetti on the front seat of the car ran counter
to the theory of the Commonwealth that Vanzetti was
at the rear. Moreover, Reed testified that "the
quality of the English [of Vanzetti] was unmistakable
and clear" (R. 329), while at the trial Vanzetti's English
was found to be so imperfect that an interpreter had
to be employed.

1. Harry E. Dolbeare testified that somewhere
between 10 and 12 A.M. he saw a car going past him
in South Braintree with five people in it, one of whom
he identified as Vanzetti: —

Q. There was nothing that attracted your attention in this
case except one man leaning forward as though he was talking
to another man? A. Yes, there was.

He then stated that there was something that attracted his
attention to this man before the car got opposite him, — it was
the appearance of the whole five that attracted his attention.
They appeared strange to him, as strangers to the town, as a
carload of foreigners. He hardly knows how to express himself. He knows how he felt at the time. "I felt it was a tough
looking bunch. That is the very feeling that came to my mind
at the time. . . . I guess that is all. That is all I recall now."

Q. And it is nothing unusual to see an automobile with three
or five or seven foreigners in it, is it? A. No.

Q. And those automobiles go through to Holbrook, to Randolph, and all through that district from the Fore River with
those workmen, don't they? A. Yes, sir.

He cannot give any description of the men who were on the front seat of the automobile. He did not take any particular notice of them. "This one man attracted my attention."

There is nothing other than what he has already given by which he characterizes these men as a tough looking bunch. He does not know whether the other two men who sat on the back seat had mustaches or beards of any kind. He does not know what kind of a hat or cap the man in the middle, who leaned forward to speak, wore. He does not know whether this man had a cap with a visor projecting out or whether he had on a slouch hat. (R. 285, 286, 287.)

2. LeVangie, the gate tender of the New Haven railroad, was on duty at the South Braintree grade crossing on the day of the murder. According to his testimony, the murder car drove up to the crossing just as he was lowering the gate, and a man inside forced him at the point of a revolver to let the car through before the advancing train. LeVangie identified Vanzetti as the man who was driving the car. LeVangie's testimony was discredited by the testimony of McCarthy, a locomotive fireman of the New Haven, who testified that three quarters of an hour after the murder he had the following conversation with Le-Vangie: —

LeVangie said "There was a shooting affair going on." I says, "Some one shot?" I says, "Who?" "Some one, a fellow got murdered." I said, "Who did it?" He said he did not know. He said there was some fellows went by in an automobile and he heard the shots, and he started to put down the gates, and as he started to put them down one of them pointed a gun at him and he left the gates alone and ducked in the shanty. I asked him if he knew them. He said, no, he did not. I asked him if he would know them again if he saw them. He said "No." He said all he could see was the gun and he ducked. (R. 1040.)

Moreover, LeVangie was discredited by all the other identification witnesses on both sides, who insisted that the driver of the car was a young, small, light-haired man, whereas Vanzetti was middle-aged, dark, with a black moustache. But, though the District Attorney had to repudiate LeVangie, he characteristically held on to LeVangie's identification. The following quotation from the District Attorney's summing up reveals the worthlessness of LeVangie's testimony; it throws no less light on the guiding attitude of the prosecution: —

They find fault, gentlemen, with Levangie. They say that Levangie is wrong in saying that Vanzetti was driving that car. I agree with them, gentlemen. I would not be trying to do justice to these defendants if I pretended that personally so far as you are concerned about my personal belief on that, that Vanzetti drove that car over the crossing. I do not believe any such thing. You must be overwhelmed with the testimony that when the car started it was driven by a light haired man who showed every indication of being sickly.

We cannot mold the testimony of witnesses, gentlemen. We have got to take them as they testify on their oath, and we put Levangie on because necessarily he must have been there. He saw something. He described a light haired man to some of the witnesses. They produced Carter, the first witness they put on, to say that he said the light haired man, — the driver was a light haired man. That is true. I believe my brothers will agree with me on that proposition, but he saw the face of Vanzetti in that car, and is his testimony to be rejected if it disagrees with everybody else if you are satisfied he honestly meant to tell the truth?

And can't you reconcile it with the possibility, no, the like-lihood or more than that, the probability that at that time Vanzetti was directly behind the driver in the quick glance this man Levangie had of the car going over when they were going up over the crossing. * * *

Right or wrong, we have to take it as it is. And I agree if it depends on the accuracy of the statement that Vanzetti was driving, then it is n't right, because I would have to reject personally the testimony of witnesses for the defense as well as for the Commonwealth who testified to the contrary. I ask you to find as a matter of commonsense he was, in the light of other witnesses, in the car, and if on the left side that he may well have been immediately behind the driver. (R. 1130–1.)

In other words, obliged to repudiate the testimony of LeVangie that Vanzetti was on the front seat, the Commonwealth urged the jury to find that although LeVangie said that Vanzetti was on the front seat, he meant he was on the back seat. At the time that he offered this testimony of LeVangie, the District Attorney had held interviews with, and had in his possession written statements of, the only two persons who had an extended opportunity to observe the driver of the car. The detailed description given by them absolutely excluded Vanzetti. (Kelly and Kennedy Affidavits, M. R. 152, 147.) The reliability of these observers and of their statements has not been chal-lenged. Yet they were not called by the District Attorney; instead he called LeVangie. Unfortunately, the existence of Kelly and Kennedy was until very recently unknown to the defense and of course, there-fore, their testimony was unavailable for Sacco and Vanzetti at the trial.

The alibi for Vanzetti was overwhelming. Thirty-one eyewitnesses testified positively that no one of the men that they saw in the murder car was Vanzetti. Thirteen witnesses either testified directly that Vanzetti was in Plymouth selling fish on the day of the murder, or furnished corroboration of such testimony.

What is the worth of identification testimony even when uncontradicted? The identification of strangers is proverbially untrustworthy. The hazards of such testimony are established by a formidable number of instances in the records of English and American trials. These instances are recent — not due to the brutalities of ancient criminal procedure. In England the case of Adolf Beck, who was twice convicted as a swindler on the confident identification of numerous witnesses but subsequently proven innocent, disclosed so serious a miscarriage of justice as to lead to the establishment of a Court of Criminal Appeals, with broad revisory powers over the action of juries and trial judges. The circumstances of the Beck case led to the appointment of a Royal Commission, headed by the Master of the Rolls, which thus expressed itself on identification testimony: —

Evidence as to identity based on personal impressions, however *bona fide*, is perhaps of all classes of evidence the least to be relied upon, and therefore, unless supported by other facts, an unsafe basis for the verdict of a jury.[1]

Since 1908, in sixteen cases the English Court of Criminal Appeals quashed convictions because of the in-

[1] Watson, *Trial of Adolf Beck*, p. 250.

sufficiency of identification.[1]   Similarly, in capital cases alone, the inadequacy of identification testimony has five times since 1914 led the New York Court of Appeals to reverse convictions.[2]

In the Sacco-Vanzetti case the elements of uncertainty were intensified. All the identifying witnesses were speaking from casual observation of men they had never seen before, men of foreign race, under circumstances of unusual confusion. Thus one witness, Cole, "thought at the first glance that Vanzetti was a Portuguese fellow named Tony that he knew." (R. 390.) Afterward he was sure the man was Vanzetti. The old song, "All Coons Look Alike to Me," represents a deep experience of human fallibility. Moreover, the methods pursued by the police in eliciting

[1] *R.* v. *Osborne*, 1 Cr. App. R. 144 (1908); *R.* v. *Bettridge*, 1 Cr. App. R. 236 (1908); *R.* v. *Smith*, 3 Cr. App. R. 87 (1909); *R.* v. *Bundy*, 5 Cr. App. R. 270 (1910); *R.* v. *Walker & Malyon*, 5 Cr. App. R. 296 (1910); *R.* v. *Witton*, 6 Cr. App. R. 149 (1911); *R.* v. *Parker*, 6 Cr. App. R. 285 (1911); *R.* v. *Chapman*, 7 Cr. App. R. 53 (1911); *R.* v. *Thompson*, 7 Cr. App. R. 203 (1912); *R.* v. *Williams*, 8 Cr. App. R. 85 (1912); *R.* v. *Varley*, 10 Cr. App. R. 125 (1914); *R.* v. *Gilling*, 12 Cr. App. R. 131 (1916); *R.* v. *Chadwick et al.*, 12 Cr. App. R. 247 (1917); *R.* v. *Murphy*, 15 Cr. App. R. 181 (1921); *R.* v. *Millichamp*, 16 Cr. App. R. 83 (1921); *R.* v. *Goss*, 17 Cr. App. R. 196 (1923).

[2] *People* v. *Jung Hing*, 212 N. Y. 393 (1914); *People* v. *De Martini*, 213 N. Y. 203 (1914); *People* v. *Seppi*, 221 N. Y. 62 (1917); *People* v. *Montesauto*, 236 N. Y. 396 (1923); *People* v. *Kvlana*, 241 N. Y. 481 (1926).

See also the case of Thomas Berdue, well known in California history. One Thomas Berdue was accused of various crimes, including murder, which were actually committed by James Stuart, a member of a famous outlaw gang. Berdue and Stuart had several similar identifying marks which led to Berdue's conviction. After his conviction, however, Stuart was caught by the famous Vigilance Committee and confessed; but even then the authorities holding Berdue were reluctant to release him. Williams, *History of the San Francisco Committee of Vigilance of 1851*, 170–6, 257–8, 303.

identification in this case fatally impair its worth. In England, such methods would have discredited the testimony and nullified a verdict based upon it. The recognized procedure is to line up the suspect with others, and so far as possible with individuals of the same race and class, so as not to provoke identification through accentuation. In defiance of these necessary safeguards, Sacco and Vanzetti after their arrest were shown singly to persons brought there for the purposes of identification, not as part of a "parade." [1] Moreover, Sacco and Vanzetti were not even allowed to be their natural selves; they were compelled to simulate the behavior of the Braintree bandits. Under such conditions identification of foreigners is a farce.[2]

[1] See *R. v. Chapman*, 7 Cr. App. R. 53 (1911), and *R. v. Williams*, 8 Cr. App. R. 84 (1912). The requirements of such a "parade" have been recently reënforced by strict rules promulgated by the Secretary of State for Home Affairs, following the disclosure of abuse even by the London police. See report of Mr. J. F. P. Rawlinson, K.C., M.P., on case of Major R. O. Sheppard, and leader thereon ("A Disquieting Report") in the London *Times*, Monday, August 17, 1925, and letter of Sir William Joynson-Hicks, the Home Secretary, to Mr. Rawlinson, with leader thereon ("Reforms in Police Procedure"), London *Times*, Friday, August 28, 1925.

[2] Two other items of evidence, relied on by the Commonwealth, seem too insignificant for detailed attention. (1) A cap was found at the scene of the murder, and the Commonwealth bent its efforts toward identifying it as a cap of Sacco's. It was a cap of no particular distinctiveness, an ordinary pepper-and-salt cap, of which hundreds of thousands are produced and worn. It fitted Sacco roughly, but was, he said, a little too small. The only evidence in support of the identification of the cap was the hesitant testimony of Sacco's employer, basing his opinion on a casual observation of a cap hanging on a nail near Sacco as he worked in the factory, that it bore a general resemblance in color to the cap in dispute. (R. 450.) He explicitly denied, however, that he meant his testimony to be identification of the cap. (R. 452.) On the other hand, there was the most specific denial, both by Sacco and Mrs. Sacco, that the cap was Sacco's cap, the denial being supported by Mrs. Sacco's explanation that her husband never

To anticipate our story, after the conviction Judge Thayer himself abandoned the identification of Sacco and Vanzetti as the ground on which the jury's verdict rested. In denying a motion for a new trial, based on the discovery of a new eyewitness with better opportunities for observation than any of the other witnesses on either side, who in his affidavit swore that Sacco was not the man in the car, Judge Thayer ruled that this evidence

would simply mean one more piece of evidence of the same kind and directed to the same end, and in my judgment, would have no effect whatever upon the verdicts. For these verdicts did not rest, in my judgment, upon the testimony of the eye witnesses, for the defendants, as it was, called more witnesses than the Commonwealth who testified that neither of the defendants were in the bandit car.

The evidence that convicted these defendants was circum-

---

wore a cap with earflaps because "he don't look good in them, positively. * * * I don't like him [in them.]" (R. 1085.)

(2) A revolver was found on Vanzetti at the time of his arrest, and there was some evidence that Berardelli had once possessed a revolver. The Commonwealth sought to prove that Berardelli's revolver was snatched from him at the time of the murder and should be identified with the one found on Vanzetti. No one could testify that Berardelli had a revolver with him at the time of the murder and no one had seen one of the murderers take it from him. Mrs. Berardelli thought her husband's revolver had a black handle like Vanzetti's, but could say no more. (R. 426.) Berardelli had taken his revolver into Boston to have the spring repaired in March 1920. An employee of the repair shop testified that in his opinion the revolver found on Vanzetti answered the general description of the revolver brought into the shop by Berardelli. There was also conflicting and inconclusive testimony concerning the hammer of the revolver. No evidence was offered to indicate that the spring in Vanzetti's revolver was new; on the contrary, there was the undisputed testimony of two experts for the defense that the spring in his revolver was no newer than any other part of it, and the defense further offered the evidence of a witness who swore that he had sold to Vanzetti the revolver found on him.

stantial and was evidence that is known in law as "consciousness of guilt." (Defendants' Bill of Exceptions to Decision on Second Supplementary Motion for New Trial, 22.)

To this "consciousness of guilt" we shall now address ourselves.

CHAPTER III

By "consciousness of guilt" Judge Thayer meant that
the conduct of Sacco and Vanzetti after April 15 was
the conduct of murderers. This inference of guilt was
drawn from their behavior on the night of May 5,
before and after arrest, and also from their possession
of firearms. It is vital to keep in mind the exact data
on which, according to Judge Thayer, these two men
are to be sentenced to death. There was no claim
whatever at the trial, and none has ever been suggested
since, that Sacco and Vanzetti had any prior experience in holdups or any previous association with bandits;
no claim that the sixteen thousand dollars taken from
the victims ever found its way into their pockets; no
claim that their financial condition, or that of Sacco's
family (he had a wife and child, and another child
was soon to be born), was in any way changed after
April 15; no claim that after the murder either Sacco
or Vanzetti changed his manner of living or employment. Not at all! Neither of these men had ever
been accused of crime before their arrest.[1] Nor, during
the three weeks between the murder and their arrest,
did they behave like men who were concealing the
crime of murder. They did not go into hiding; they
did not abscond with the spoils; they did not live under
assumed names. On the contrary they maintained

[1] See footnote, p. 7.

their old lodgings; they pursued openly their callings, within a few miles of the town where they were supposed to have committed murders in broad daylight; and when arrested Sacco was found to have in his pocket an announcement of a forthcoming meeting at which Vanzetti was to speak.[1] Was this the behavior of men eluding identification?

What, then, was the evidence against them?

1. Sacco and Vanzetti, as we have seen, were two of four Italians who called for Boda's car at Johnson's garage on the evening of May 5. It will be remembered that in pursuance of a prearranged plan Mrs. Johnson, under pretext of having to fetch some milk, went to a neighbor's house to telephone the police. Mrs. Johnson testified that the two defendants followed her to the house on the opposite side of the street and when, after telephoning, she reappeared they followed her back. (R. 361.) Thereafter the men, having been advised by Mr. Johnson not to run the car without the current year's number plate, left without it: —

Q. Now, Boda came there to get his car, did n't he? A. Yes.

Q. There were no 1920 number plates on it? A. No.

Q. You advised him not to take the car and run it without the 1920 number plates, did n't you? A. Yes.

[1] The manifesto ran as follows: —
"You have fought all the wars. You have worked for all the capitalists. You have wandered over all the countries. Have you harvested the fruits of your labors, the price of your victories? Does the past comfort you? Does the present smile on you? Does the future promise you anything? Have you found a piece of land where you can live like a human being and die like a human being? On these questions, on this argument, and on this theme, the struggle for existence, Bartolomeo Vanzetti will speak. Hour —— day —— hall ——. Admission free. Freedom of discussion to all. Take the ladies with you." (R. 1124.)

Q. And he accepted your view?   A. He seemed to.
Q. He seemed to.   And after some conversation went away?
A. Yes.   (R. 378.)

This was the whole of the testimony on the strength
of which Judge Thayer put the following question to
the jury: —

Did the defendants, in company with Orciani and Boda,
leave the Johnson house because the automobile had no 1920
number plate on it, or because they were conscious of or became suspicious of what Mrs. Johnson did in the Bartlett
house? If they left because they had no 1920 number plates
on the automobile, then you may say there was no consciousness of guilt in consequence of their sudden departure, but if
they left because they were consciously guilty [1] of what was
being done by Mrs. Johnson in the Bartlett house, then you
may say that is evidence tending to prove consciousness of
guilt on their part. (R. 1156.)

2. Following their departure from the Johnson house,
Sacco and Vanzetti were arrested by a policeman who
boarded their street car as it was coming into Brockton.
Three policemen testified as to their behavior after
being taken into custody: —

[As to Vanzetti] He went down through the car and when
he got opposite to the seat he stopped and he asked them where
they were from. "They said 'Bridgewater.' I said, 'What was
you doing in Bridgewater?' They said 'We went down to see
a friend of mine.' I said, 'Who is your friend?' He said, 'A
man by the — they call him "Poppy."' 'Well,' I said, 'I
want you, you are under arrest.' Vanzetti was sitting on the
inside of the seat."

Q. When you say "on the inside," you mean toward the

[1] These are Judge Thayer's words. His meaning must, presumably,
have been "guiltily conscious."

aisle or toward the window? A. Toward the window. The inside of the car; and he went, put his hand in his hip pocket and I says, "Keep your hands out on your lap, or you will be sorry."

THE DEFENDANT VANZETTI. You are a liar! (R. 393.)

[As to Sacco] I told them when we started that the first false move I would put a bullet in them. On the way up to the Station Sacco reached his hand to put under his overcoat and I told him to keep his hands out side of his clothes and on his lap.

Q. Will you illustrate to the jury how he placed his hand? A. He was sitting down with his hands that way (indicating), and he moved his hand up to put it in under his overcoat.

Q. At what point? A. Just about the stomach there, across his waistband, and I says to him, "Have you got a gun there?" He says "No." He says, "I ain't got no gun." "Well," I says, "Keep your hands outside of your clothes." We went along a little further and he done the same thing. I gets up on my knees on the front seat and I reaches over and I puts my hand under his coat but I did not see any gun. "Now," I says, "Mister, if you put your hand in there again, you are going to get into trouble." He says, "I don't want no trouble." (R. 394.)

3. In statements made to the District Attorney and to the Chief of Police, at the police station after their arrest, both Sacco and Vanzetti lied. By misstatements they tried to conceal their movements on the day of their arrest, the friends they had been to see, the places they had visited. For instance, Vanzetti denied that he knew Boda.

What of this evidence of "consciousness of guilt"? The testimony of the police that Sacco and Vanzetti were about to draw pistols was emphatically denied by them. These denials, it was urged, were confirmed by the inherent probabilities of the situation. Did

Sacco and Vanzetti upon arrest reveal the qualities of the perpetrators of the Braintree murders? Those crimes were committed by desperadoes — men whose profession it was to take life if necessary and who freely used guns to hold bystanders at bay in order to make their "get-away." Is there the slightest likeness between the behavior of the Braintree bandits and the behavior of Sacco and Vanzetti, when the two were arrested by one policeman? Would the ready and ruthless gunmen at Braintree so quietly have surrendered themselves into custody on a capital charge of which they knew themselves to be guilty? If Sacco and Vanzetti were the holdup men of Braintree, why did they not draw upon their expert skill and attempt to make their escape by scattering shots? But, if not "gunmen," why should Sacco and Vanzetti have carried guns? The possession of firearms in this country has not at all the significance that it would have, say, in England. The extensive carrying of guns by people who are not "gunmen" is a matter of common knowledge. The widespread advertisement of firearms indicates that we may not unfairly be described as a gun-carrying people. The practice is unfortunately rife for a variety of reasons. Sacco and Vanzetti had credible reasons, wholly unrelated to professional banditry. Sacco acquired the habit of carrying a pistol while a night watchman because, as his employer testified, "night watchmen protecting property do have guns." (R. 458.) Vanzetti carried a revolver, "because it was a very bad time, and I like to have a revolver for self defense": —

Q. How much money did you use to carry around with you?
A. When I went to Boston for fish, I can carry eighty, one hundred dollars, one hundred and twenty dollars.

There were many crimes, many hold-ups, many robberies at that time. (R. 829.)

The other evidence from which "consciousness of guilt" was drawn the two Italians admitted. Sacco and Vanzetti acknowledged that they behaved in the way described by Mrs. Johnson, and freely conceded that when questioned at the police station they told lies. What was their explanation of this conduct? To exculpate themselves of the crime of murder they had to disclose elaborately their guilt of radicalism. In order to meet the significance which the prosecution attached to the incidents at the Johnson house and those following, it became necessary for the defendants to advertise to the jury their offensive views, and thereby to excite the deepest prejudices of a Norfolk County jury, picked for its respectability and sitting in judgment upon two men of alien blood and abhorrent philosophy.

Innocent men, it is said, do not lie when picked up by the police. But Sacco and Vanzetti knew they were not innocent of the charge on which they *supposed* themselves arrested, and about which the police interrogated them. For when apprehended they were not confronted with the charge of murder; they were not accused of banditry; they were not given the remotest intimation that the murders of Parmenter and Berardelli were laid at their door. They were told they were arrested as "suspicious characters" (R. 393), and the meaning which that carried to their minds was rendered concrete by the questions that were put to them: —

(As to Vanzetti) Did you tell Mr. Katzmann the truth about Pappi and why you — A. About Pappi, yes, but I don't say that I was there to take the automobile and I don't speak about the literature . . . I don't tell him about the meeting on next Sunday. Yes, I told them, I explained to them the meeting, I think.

Q. Tell us all you recall that Stewart, the chief, asked of you? A. He asked me why we were in Bridgewater, how long I know Sacco, if I am a Radical, if I am an anarchist or Communist, and he asked me if I believe in the government of the United States. (R. 839.)

Q. Did either Chief Stewart at the Brockton police station or Mr. Katzmann tell you that you were suspected of robberies and murder? A. No.

Q. Was there any question asked of you or any statement made to you to indicate to you that you were charged with that crime on April 15th? A. No.

Q. What did you understand, in view of the questions asked of you, what did you understand you were being detained for at the Brockton police station? A. I understand they arrested me for a political matter. * * *

Q. * * * Why did you feel you were being detained for political opinions? A. Because I was asked if I was a Socialist. I said, "Well, — "

Q. You mean by reason of the questions asked of you? A. Because I was asked if I am a Socialist, if I am I. W. W., if I am a Communist, if I am a Radical, if I am a Blackhand. (R. 883–4.)

(As to Sacco) What did you think was the time when the crime that you were arrested for had been committed? A. I never think anything else than Radical.

Q. What? A. To the Radical arrest, you know, the way

they do in New York, the way they arrest so many people there.

Q. What made you think that? A. Because I was not registered, and I was working for the movement for the working class, for the laboring class. (R. 903–4.)

Q. What occurred with Mr. Stewart [Chief of Police] that made you think you were being held for Radical activities? A. Well, because the first thing they asked me if I was an anarchist, a communist or socialist. (R. 1016.)

Plainly their arrest meant to Sacco and Vanzetti arrest for radicalism. That being so, why should they evade police inquiries; what fear governed them in making lies to escape that charge?

The early winter of 1919–20 saw the beginning of an elaborately planned campaign by the Department of Justice under Attorney-General Mitchell Palmer for the wholesale arrest and deportation of "Reds" — aliens under suspicion of sympathy with the Communist régime. The details of these raids, their brutality and their lawlessness, are set forth authoritatively in decisions of United States courts condemning the misconduct of the Department of Justice. These findings the Attorney-General never ventured to have reviewed by the higher courts.[1]

[1] In *Colyer* v. *Skeffington*, about a dozen aliens brought habeas corpus for relief from deportation orders against them on the ground that the proceedings of which they were the victims were denials of that due process of law which is guaranteed even to aliens by the Constitution. Upon the facts before him, consisting largely of official documents of instruction issued by the Department of Justice and of the testimony of agents of the Department, the Court found that these aliens were denied their constitutional rights and he therefore discharged them. From these findings and the order discharging the aliens, the Government never appealed. This failure to seek review in the higher courts was a clear confession of guilt for the outrages of lawlessness established in *Colyer* v. *Skeffington*. For the failure

Boston was one of the worst centres of this lawlessness and hysteria. Its proximity to industrial communities having a large proportion of foreign labor and a history of past ugly industrial conflicts lent to the lawless activities of the government officials the widespread support of influential public opinion.[1] One of the leading citizens of Boston, Mr. John F. Moors, himself a banker, has called attention to the fact that "the hysteria against 'the reds' was so great, at the time when these men were convicted, that even the most substantial bankers in this city [Boston] were carried away to the extent of paying for full-page advertisements about the red peril." [2] Sacco and Vanzetti were notorious Reds. They were associates of

---

to appeal on these issues was emphasized by the fact that the Government did appeal in five other cases raising totally different questions, issues as to the meaning of a statute and not at all as to official lawlessness. (*Colyer* v. *Skeffington*, 265 Fed. 17, reversed as to some aliens only in *Skeffington* v. *Katzeff*, 277 Fed. 129.)

See Report upon the Illegal Practices of the United States Department of Justice by Roscoe Pound *et al.* (May 1920) which former Justice Charles E. Hughes thus summarized: "Very recently information has been laid by responsible citizens at the bar of public opinion of violations of personal rights which savor of the worst practices of tyranny." (Address at Centennial Celebration of Harvard Law School, June 21, 1920.)

[1] In 1923 Mr. Moorfield Storey thus characterized the situation: " * * * on a small scale a 'reign of terror' [was produced] in which some thousands of innocent people were very cruelly treated and exposed to much suffering and loss * * *. The safeguards of the Constitution were ignored, and any true American must blush at what was done and the indifference with which he and all but a handful of his countrymen tolerated it." (Introduction to Post, *Deportations Delirium*, xii–xiii.) Compare with this Mr. Storey's letter in the *Boston Herald* for October 27, 1926, arguing, in support of the Sacco-Vanzetti verdict, the conceded strength of the Massachusetts system of administering the criminal law under ordinary circumstances.

[2] Letter in the *Boston Herald*, November 3, 1926.

leading radicals. They had for some time been on the list of suspects of the Department of Justice, and were especially obnoxious because they were draft-dodgers.

The press made them daily anxious for their safety. The newspapers, it will be recalled, were filled with lurid accounts of what the Reds had done and were planning, and equally lurid accounts of the methods of the Government in dealing with the Reds. Not only were Sacco and Vanzetti living in this enveloping atmosphere of apprehension; the terrorizing methods of the Government had very specific meaning for them. Two of their friends had already been deported. Deportation, they knew, meant not merely expulsion and uprooting from home. What it did mean they had just learned. Among Vanzetti's radical group in Boston the arrest of the New York radical Salsedo, and his detention incommunicado by the Department of Justice, had been for some weeks a source of great concern. Vanzetti was sent to New York by this group to confer with the Italian Defense Committee having charge of the case of Salsedo and all other Italian political prisoners. On his return, May 2, he reported to his Boston friends the advice which had been given to the Italian Defense Committee by their New York lawyer: to dispose of their radical literature and thus eliminate the most damaging evidence in the deportation proceedings they feared.

THE WITNESS [Sacco]. Vanzetti come into the hall. He told us we are to get ready and advise our friends, any friend who knows a friend as a Socialist and active in the movement of labor, why, they are advised to get the books and literature to put at some place and hide not to find by the police or the state. And another thing he says nobody know why they arrest Salsedo and Elia.

THE COURT. Nobody knows —

THE WITNESS. Why, for what charge they did arrest Salsedo and Elia and Cammiti, and some of the other fellows before. So they say after all over in New York, a spy to find out the Radicals and they find out the same, the money, all the friends that been sending from Massachusetts and all over New England, been sending the money for the defending of Salsedo and Elia, — who is the man receiving it, who is the man responsible for those things, so we decided and Vanzetti decided it was same time, the quicker we come and get literature and anything out of the Radical's house, the Socialists, and to hide it. That is all he said. That is why I remembered. He probably said some more, but I could not remember all the conversation we had, because he been talking an hour, pretty near an hour and a half, and I could not remember all he says. (R. 907.)

The urgency of acting on this advice was intensified by the tragic news of Salsedo's death after Vanzetti's return from New York. It was to carry out this advice that Vanzetti and his friends were trying to get Boda's car from Johnson's garage on May 5. The day before had come the news of Salsedo's death.

Q. Any one time you mentioned that you were afraid, what did you mean by that? A. I mean that I was afraid, for I know that my friends there in New York have jumped down from the jail in the street and killed himself. The papers say that he jump down, but we don't know.

Q. You now allude to who? Who is that man? A. Salsedo.

Q. When did you learn of Salsedo's death? A. On the day, in the day, fourth, 4th of May. (R. 881.)

Though Salsedo's death was unexplained, to Sacco and Vanzetti it conveyed only one explanation. It was a symbol of their fears and perhaps an omen of their own fate.

Let us now resume the story of the trial. The witnesses for the Commonwealth had dealt with identification of men and of bullets, and the suspicious conduct of Sacco and Vanzetti at the time of arrest. On the witness stand Sacco and Vanzetti accounted for their movements on April 15. They also accounted for their ambiguous behavior on May 5. Up to the time that Sacco and Vanzetti testified to their radical activities, their pacifism and their flight to Mexico to escape the draft, the trial was a trial for murder and banditry; with the cross-examination of Sacco and Vanzetti patriotism and radicalism became the dominant emotional issues. Of course, these were not the technical issues which were left to the jury. But, as Mr. Justice Holmes has admonished us, "in spite of forms [juries] are extremely likely to be impregnated by the environing atmosphere." [1] Outside the courtroom the Red hysteria was rampant; it was allowed to dominate within. The prosecutor systematically played on the feelings of the jury by exploiting the unpatriotic and despised beliefs of Sacco and Vanzetti, and the judge allowed him thus to divert and pervert the jury's mind. Only a detailed knowledge of the conduct of the prosecutor, sanctioned by the Court, can give an adequate realization of the extent to which prejudice, instead of being rigorously excluded, was systematically fostered.

[1] *Frank* v. *Mangum*, 237 U. S. at 349.

The opening question on cross-examination of Vanzetti by the District Attorney discloses a motif that he persistently played upon: —

Q. (By Mr. Katzmann) So you left Plymouth, Mr. Vanzetti, in May, 1917, to dodge the draft, did you? A. Yes, sir. * * *

Q. When this country was at war, you ran away, so you would not have to fight as a soldier? A. Yes. (R. 842–3.)

Q. You were going to advise in a public meeting men who had gone to war? Are you that man? A. Yes, sir, I am that man, not the man you want me, but I am that man. (R. 865–6.)

This method was elaborated when Sacco took the stand: —

Q. (By Mr. Katzmann) Did you say yesterday you love a free country? A. Yes, sir.

Q. Did you love this country in the month of May, 1917? A. I did not say, — I don't want to say I did not love this country.

Q. Did you love this country in that month of 1917? A. If you can, Mr. Katzmann, if you give me that, — I could explain —

Q. Do you understand that question? A. Yes.

Q. Then will you please answer it? A. I can't answer in one word.

Q. You can't say whether you loved the United States of America one week before the day you enlisted for the first draft? A. I can't say in one word, Mr. Katzmann. (R. 919.)

Q. Did you love this country in the last week of May, 1917? A. That is pretty hard for me to say in one word, Mr. Katzmann.

Q. There are two words you can use, Mr. Sacco, yes or no. Which one is it? A. Yes.

Q. And in order to show your love for this United States of America when she was about to call upon you to become a soldier you ran away to Mexico. (R. 919.)

Q. Did you go to Mexico to avoid being a soldier for this country that you loved? A. Yes. (R. 920.)

Q. And would it be your idea of showing your love for your wife that when she needed you, you ran away from her? A. I did not run away from her.

MR. MOORE. I object.

THE WITNESS. I was going to come after if I need her.

THE COURT. He may answer. Simply on the question of credibility, that is all.

Q. Would it be your idea of love for your wife that you were to run from her when she needed you?

MR. JEREMIAH MCANARNEY. Pardon me. I ask for an exception on that.

THE COURT. Excluded. One may not run away. He had not admitted he ran away.

Q. Then I will ask you, did n't you run away from Milford so as to avoid being a soldier for the United States? A. I did not run away.

Q. You mean you walked away? A. Yes.

Q. You don't understand me when I say "run away," do you? A. That is vulgar.

Q. That is vulgar? A. You can say a little intelligent, Mr. Katzmann.

Q. Don't you think going away from your country is a vulgar thing to do when she needs you? A. I don't believe in war.

Q. You don't believe in war? A. No, sir.

Q. Do you think it is a cowardly thing to do what you did? A. No, sir.

Q. Do you think it is a brave thing to do what you did? A. Yes, sir.

Q. Do you think it would be a brave thing to go away from your own wife? A. No.

Q. When she needed you? A. No. (R. 920-1.)

Q. Why did n't you stay there, down there in that free country, and work with a pick and shovel? A. I don't think

I did sacrifice to learn a job to go to pick and shovel in Mexico.

Q. Is it because, — is your love for the United States of America commensurate with the amount of money you can get in this country per week? A. Better conditions, yes.

Q. Better country to make money, is n't it? A. Yes. * * *

Q. Is your love for this country measured by the amount of money you can earn here? * * * A. I never loved money. (R. 921–2.)

Q. Is standing by a country when she needs a soldier evidence of love of country?

MR. JEREMIAH McANARNEY. That I object to, if your Honor please. And I might state now I want my objection to go to this whole line of interrogation.

THE COURT. I think you opened it up.

MR. JEREMIAH McANARNEY. No, if your Honor please, I have not.

THE COURT. It seems to me you have. Are you going to claim much of all the collection of the literature and the books was really in the interest of the United States as well as these people and therefore it has opened up the credibility of the defendant when he claims that all that work was done really for the interest of the United States in getting his literature out of the way?

MR. JEREMIAH McANARNEY. That claim is not presented in anything tantamount to the language just used by the Court, and in view of the record as it stands at this time I object to this line of inquiry.

THE COURT. Is that not your claim, that the defendant, as a reason that he has given for going to the Johnson house, that they wanted the automobile to prevent people from being deported and to get this literature all out of the way? Does he not claim that that was done in the interest of the United States, to prevent violation of the law by the distribution of this literature? I understood that was the —

MR. JEREMIAH McANARNEY. Are you asking that as a question to me?

THE COURT. Yes.

MR. JEREMIAH McANARNEY. Absolutely we have taken no such position as that, and the evidence at this time does not warrant the assumption of that question. (R. 924-5.)

THE COURT. Are you going to claim that what the defendant did was in the interest of the United States?

MR. JEREMIAH McANARNEY. Your Honor please, I now object to your Honor's statement as prejudicial to the rights of the defendants and ask that this statement be withdrawn from the jury.

THE COURT. There is no prejudicial remark made that I know of, and none were intended. I simply asked you, sir, whether you propose to offer evidence as to what you said to me.

MR. JEREMIAH McANARNEY. If your Honor please, the remarks made with reference to the country and whether the acts that he was doing were for the benefit of the country. I can see no other inference to be drawn from those except prejudicial to the defendants. * * *

THE COURT. All I ask is this one question, and it will simplify matters very much. Is it your claim that in the collection of the literature and the books and papers that that was done in the interest of the United States?

MR. JEREMIAH McANARNEY. No, I make no such broad claim as that. * * *

MR. KATZMANN. Well, he [Sacco] stated in his direct examination yesterday that he loved a free country, and I offer it to attack that statement made in his examination by his own counsel.

THE COURT. That is what I supposed, and that is what I supposed that remark meant when it was introduced in this cross-examination, but counsel now say they don't make that claim.

MR. KATZMANN. They say they don't make the claim that gathering up the literature on May 5th at West Bridgewater was for the purpose of helping the country, but that is a different mattter, not released [*sic*] to May 5th.

THE COURT. I will let you inquire further first as to what he meant by the expression. (R. 926–7.)

What did you mean when you said yesterday you loved a free country? A. Give me a chance to explain.

Q. I am asking you to explain now. A. When I was in Italy, a boy, I was a Republican, so I always thinking Republican has more chance to manage education, develop, to build some day his family, to raise the child and education, if you could. But that was my opinion; so when I came to this country I saw there was not what I was thinking before, but there was all the difference, because I been working in Italy not so hard as I been work in this country. I could live free there just as well. Work in the same condition but not so hard, about seven or eight hours a day, better food. I mean genuine. Of course, over here is good food, because it is bigger country, to any those who got money to spend, not for the working and laboring class, and in Italy is more opportunity to laborer to eat vegetable, more fresh, and I came in this country. When I been started work here very hard and been work thirteen years, hard worker, I could not been afford much a family the way I did have the idea before. I could not put any money in the bank; I could no push my boy some to go to school and other things. I teach over here men who is with me. The free idea gives any man a chance to profess his own idea, not the supreme idea, not to give any person, not to be like Spain in position, yes, about twenty centuries ago, but to give a chance to print and education, literature, free speech, that I see it was all wrong. I could see the best men, intelligent, education, they been arrested and sent to prison and died in prison for years and years without getting them out, and Debs, one of the great men in his country, he is in prison, still away in prison, because he is a Socialist. He wanted the laboring class to have better conditions and better living, more education, give a push his son if he could have a chance some day, but they put him in prison. Why? Because the capitalist class, they know, they are against that, because the capitalist class,

they don't want our child to go to high school or college or
Harvard College. There would be no chance, there would not
be no, — they don't want the working class educationed; they
want the working class to be a low all the times, be underfoot,
and not to be up with the head. So, sometimes, you see, the
Rockefellers, Morgans, they give fifty, — I mean they give five
hundred thousand dollars to Harvard College, they give a
million dollars for another school. Everyday say, "Well,
D. Rockefeller is a great man, the best man in the country."
I want to ask him who is going to Harvard College? What
benefit the working class they will get by those million dollars
they give by Rockefeller, D. Rockefellers. They won't get, the
poor class, they won't have no chance to go to Harvard College
because men who is getting $21 a week or $30 a week, I don't
care if he gets $80 a week, if he gets a family of five children
he can't live and send his child and go to Harvard College if
he wants to eat everything nature will give him. If he wants
to eat like a cow, and that is the best thing but I want men
to live like men. I like men to get everything that nature will
give best, because they belong, — we are not the friend of any
other place, but we are belong to nations. So that is why my
idea has been changed. So that is why I love people who labor
and work and see better conditions every day develop, makes
no more war. We no want fight by the gun, and we don't
want to destroy young men. The mother been suffering for
building the young man. Some day need a little more bread,
so when the time the mother get some bread or profit out of
that boy, the Rockefellers, Morgans, and some of the peoples,
high class, they send to war. Why? What is war? The war
is not shoots like Abraham Lincoln's and Abe Jefferson, to
fight for the free country, for the better education to give
chance to any other peoples, not the white people but the
black and the others, because they believe and know they are
mens like the rest, but they are war for the great millionaire.
No war for the civilization of men. They are war for business,
million dollars come on the side. What right we have to kill

each other? I been work for the Irish. I have been working with the German fellow, with the French, many other peoples. I love them people just as I could love my wife, and my people for that did receive me. Why should I go kill them men? What he done to me? He never done anything, so I don't believe in no war. I want to destroy those guns. All I can say, the Government put the literature, give us educations. I remember in Italy, a long time ago, about sixty years ago, I should say, yes, about sixty years ago, the Government they could not control very much those two, — devilment went on, and robbery, so one of the government in the cabinet he says, "If you want to destroy those devilments, if you want to take off all those criminals, you ought to give a chance to Socialist literature, education of people, emancipation. That is why I destroy governments, boys." That is why my idea I love Socialists. That is why I like people who want education and living, building, who is good, just as much as they could. That is all.

Q. And that is why you love the United States of America? A. Yes.

Q. She is back more than twenty centuries like Spain, is she? A. At the time of the war they do it. (R. 927–9.)

Q. Do you remember speaking of educational advantages before the recess? A. Yes, sir.

Q. Do you remember speaking of Harvard University? A. Yes, sir.

Q. Do you remember saying that you could not get an education there unless you had money? I do not mean you used those exact words. I do not contend you did, but, in substance, did n't you say that? A. They have to use money in the rule of the Government.

Q. No. You don't understand. Did you hear it, perhaps? A. I can't understand.

Q. I will raise my voice a little bit. Did you say in substance you could not send your boy to Harvard? A. Yes.

Q. Unless you had money. Did you say that? A. Of course.

Q. Do you think that is true?   A. I think it is.

Q. Don't you know Harvard University educates more boys of poor people free than any other university in the United States of America?   [The Court having overruled his counsel's objection, Sacco answered.]   A. I can't answer that question, no.

Q. So without the light of knowledge on that subject, you are condemning even Harvard University, are you, as being a place for rich men?   * * *

Q. Did you intend to condemn Harvard College?   [Objection overruled.]   A. No, sir.

Q. Were you ready to say none but the rich could go there without knowing about offering scholarships?   [Objection overruled.]   A. Yes.

Q. Does your boy go to the public schools?   A. Yes.

Q. Are there any schools in the town you came from in Italy that compare with the school your boy goes to?   [Objection.]

Q. Does your boy go to the public school?   A. Yes.

Q. Without payment of money?   A. Yes.

Q. Have you free nursing where you come from in Stoughton?   A. What do you mean?

Q. A district nurse?   A. For the boys?

Q. For anybody in your family who is ill?   A. I could not say.   Yes, I never have them in my house.

Q. Do you know how many children the city of Boston is educating in the public schools? — [Objection.] free?

Q. Do you know?   A. I can't answer yes or no.

Q. Do you know it is close to one hundred thousand children?   [Objection.]   A. I know millions of people don't go there.

Mr. Jeremiah McAnarney.   Wait.   When there is objection, don't answer.   I object to that question.

The Court.   He says he does n't know.

Mr. Jeremiah McAnarney.   I object to that answer.   I object to the question and the answer.

The Court.   The question may stand, and the answer also.

Mr. Jeremiah McAnarney.   Will your Honor save an exception?   (R. 931–2.)

Q. The question is this: As far as you understood Fruzetti's views, were yours the same?   [Objection overruled.]

Q. Answer please.   A. (Through the interpreter) I cannot say yes or no.

Q. Is it because you can't or because you don't want to? A. (Through the interpreter) Because it is a very delicate question.

Q. It is very delicate, isn't it, because he was deported for his views?   (R. 939.)

Q. Do you know why Fruzetti was deported?   A. (Through the interpreter) Yes.

Q. Was it because he was of anarchistic opinions?

The Interpreter.   He says he understands it now.

Q. Was it because Fruzetti entertained anarchistic opinions? A. One reason, he was an anarchist. Another reason, Fruzetti been writing all the time on the newspapers, and I am not sure why the reason he been deported. * * *

Q. Was Fruzetti, before deportation, a subscriber to the same papers that you had in your house on May 5th?   A. Probably he is.   [Objection.] * * *

Q. Who was the other man that you said was deported from Bridgewater?   A. I did not say; I am sure there is another man been deported, but I do not know the name.

Q. See if I can refresh your recollection.   Was it Ferruccio Coacci?   A. He is one.   There is another one.

Q. Who was the other man?   A. I do not remember the name.   (R. 940.)

Q. Did you believe that they had in their homes books similar to the ones you had in your house?   A. Yes.

Q. And the books which you intended to collect were books relating to anarchy, weren't they?   A. Not all of them.

Q. How many of them?   A. Well, all together.   We are Socialists, democratic, any other socialistic information, Socialists, Syndicalists, Anarchists, any paper.

Q. Bolshevist?   A. I do not know what Bolshevism means.

Q. Soviet?   A. I do not know what Soviet means.

Q. Communism?   A. Yes.   I got some on astronomy, too. (R. 941.)

Q. You were n't going to destroy them?   A. I was going to keep them.

Q. You were going to keep them and when the time was over, you were going to bring them out again, were n't you?   A. Yes.

Q. And you were going to distribute circulars?   A. Education literature.

Q. And you were going to distribute circulars, were n't you? A. It cost money to sacrifice.

Q. You were going to distribute those papers, were n't you?

MR. JEREMIAH MCANARNEY.   The question, were you?

Q. Were you?   A. What do you mean, destroy?

Q. No, not destroy them.   After the time had gone by, were you going to bring them out, going to distribute the knowledge contained in them?   A. Certainly, because they are educational for book, educational.

Q. An education in anarchy, was n't it?   A. Why, certainly. Anarchistic is not criminals.

Q. I did n't ask you if they are criminals or not.   Nor are you to pass upon that, sir.   Was it equally true as to the books and papers and periodicals that you expected to pick up at your friends' houses, that they were not to be destroyed? A. Just to keep them, hide them.

Q. And then bring them forth afterwards when the time was over?   A. I suppose so.   (R. 941–2.)

Q. And you are a man who tells this jury that the United States of America is a disappointment to you?

MR. JEREMIAH MCANARNEY.   Wait a minute.   I object.

MR. KATZMANN.   On the question of intelligence, if your Honor please.

THE COURT.   Not quite, and you assume, too.

MR. KATZMANN.   I assumed on the question of intelligence?

THE COURT.   You assumed "you are the man."

Mr. Katzmann. "Are you the man?" That this man passed judgment on the United States of America?

Mr. Jeremiah McAnarney. I object.

The Court. He may answer, yes or no.

Mr. Jeremiah McAnarney. Will your Honor save an exception to the question and the answer?

The Court. Certainly.

Q. Are you, Mr. Sacco? A. I don't, — I can't understand this word.

Q. "Passed judgment?" A. Yes, sir.

Q. Well, told us about how disappointed you were, and what you did not find and what you expected to find. Are you that man? A. Yes. (R. 972–3.)

In the Anglo-American system of criminal procedure the rôle of a public prosecutor is very different from that of an advocate in a private cause. In the words of a leading New York case: —

> Language which might be permitted to counsel in summing up a civil action cannot with propriety be used by a public prosecutor, who is a *quasi*-judicial officer, representing the People of the state, and presumed to act impartially in the interest only of justice. If he lays aside the impartiality that should characterize his official action to become a heated partisan, and by vituperation of the prisoner and appeals to prejudice seeks to procure a conviction at all hazards, he ceases to properly represent the public interest, which demands no victim, and asks no conviction through the aid of passion, sympathy or resentment.[1]

And the language of the Lord Chief Justice in a recent English case indicates the restraint which the "quasi-judicial" character of that office should impose upon counsel for the Crown: —

[1] *People* v. *Fielding*, 158 N. Y. 542, 547 (1899).

One so often hears questions put to witnesses by counsel which are really of the nature of an invitation to an argument. You have, for instance, such questions as this: "I suggest to you that . . ." or "Is your evidence to be taken as suggesting that . . . ?" If the witness were a prudent person he would say, with the highest degree of politeness: "What you suggest is no business of mine. I am not here to make any suggestions at all. I am here only to answer relevant questions. What the conclusions to be drawn from my answers are is not for me, and as for suggestions, I venture to leave those to others." An answer of that kind, no doubt, requires a good deal of sense and self-restraint and experience, and the mischief of it is, if made, it might very well prejudice the witness with the jury, because the jury, not being aware of the consequences to which such questions might lead, might easily come to the conclusion (and it might be true) that the witness had something to conceal. It is right to remember in all such cases that the witness in the box is an amateur and the counsel who is asking questions is, as a rule, a professional conductor of argument, and it is not right that the wits of the one should be pitted against the wits of the other in the field of suggestion and controversy. What is wanted from the witness is answers to questions of fact.

One even hears questions such as: "Do you ask the jury then to believe . . . ?" The witness may very well reply: "I am asking the jury nothing; my business is to tell whatever is relevant that I know and that I am asked to tell, and therefore my answer to your question and to all such questions is 'No, I do not.'" * * * Counsel for the prosecution should refrain from [such questions] for reasons of fairness, because the Crown has no interest whatever in securing a conviction. Its sole interest is to convict the right man.[1]

In 1921 the temper of the times made it the special duty of a prosecutor and a court, engaged in trying two Italian radicals before a jury of native New

[1] *R.* v. *Baldwin*, 18 Cr. App. R. 175, 178 (1925).

Englanders, to keep the instruments of justice free from the infection of passion or prejudice: —

On these dates [1918] it was not necessary to inflame the passions of jurors by talking about the enemies of our country, rather was it a time to caution jurors against allowing their prejudices and patriotism from swaying their judgment. But the Assistant United States Attorney so far transcended his duty as a prosecuting officer that we are clearly of the opinion that the conviction of the defendant ought not to stand. The language used speaks for itself. It must have produced a situation in the minds of the jurors that destroyed a calm consideration of the rights of the defendant. The United States cannot afford to convict her citizens in this manner.[1]

In the case of Sacco and Vanzetti no such restraints were respected. By systematic exploitation of the defendants' alien blood, their imperfect knowledge of English, their unpopular social views, and their opposition to the war, the District Attorney invoked against them a riot of political passion and patriotic sentiment; and the trial judge connived at — one had almost written, coöperated in — the process. One instance out of many must here suffice. The reader will recall the colloquy between the Court and counsel which took place immediately before Sacco's long speech to the jury. Upon this conduct of Judge Thayer Mr. William G. Thompson, in his argument on appeal, made this eminently just comment: —

The persistent attempt of the Court in the presence of the jury to suggest that the defendants were claiming that the suppression of the Socialist literature was "in the interest of the United States," to which exception was taken, was even more

[1] *August* v. *United States*, 257 Fed. 388, 393 (1919).

objectionable and prejudicial. It seems incredible that the
Court could have believed from any testimony that had been
given by Vanzetti or Sacco that their purpose in collecting and
suppressing the Socialist literature had anything to do with the
interest of the United States. *If anything had been made plain,
it was that they were actuated by personal fear of sharing the fate
of Salsedo, not merely deportation, but death by violence while
awaiting deportation.* Yet the Court eight times, in the face of
as many explicit disclaimers from Mr. McAnarney, suggested
that that was the defendants' claim. Had that claim been made
it would, of course, have been the grossest hypocrisy, and might
well have sealed the fate of both defendants with the jury. The
repeated suggestion of the Court in the presence of the jury
that that *was* the claim amounted to a violation by the Court
of the defendants' elementary constitutional right to a fair and
impartial trial. It was not cured by the Court's disclaimer
made immediately after the exception was taken to the effect
that he did not intend "to prejudice the rights of either of these
defendants." Whatever the Court intended, he had fatally
prejudiced their right to a fair trial, and no general disclaimer
could undo the harm. (Brief for Defendants on first appeal
before Supreme Judicial Court, 112.)

That the real purpose of this line of the prosecutor's
cross-examination was to inflame the jury's passions
is revealed by the professed ground on which, with
the Court's sanction, it was conducted. The Commonwealth claimed that Sacco and Vanzetti's alleged
anxiety on the evening of their arrest, and the lies
they told, could only be explained by the fact that
they were the murderers of Parmenter and Berardelli.
The defense replied that their conduct was clearly
accounted for by the fact that the men were Reds,
in terror of the Department of Justice. To test the
credibility of this answer the District Attorney pro-

posed to examine Sacco and Vanzetti to find out
whether they were really radicals or only pretending
to be. It was on this theory that the Court allowed
the cross-examination.[1] The Commonwealth undertook to show that the defendants were impostors,
that they were spurious Reds. In fact, it made not
the least attempt to do so. It never disputed their
radicalism; it could not be disputed, certainly not by
Mr. Katzmann. For we now know he had been in
close connection with the Department of Justice
before the trial, and well knew that Sacco and Vanzetti were bona fide Reds, sought as such by the Government. Instead of undermining the claim of the

---

[1] This was the theory on which in its argument before the Supreme
Judicial Court the Commonwealth justified the cross-examination of Sacco:
"* * * the presiding judge could do no more than to give the District
Attorney full opportunity and latitude to develop this field of inquiry to
see whether Sacco's radical views and radical actions were real or feigned to
meet this serious inference of guilt which arose from his falsehoods." (Brief
for Commonwealth on first appeal before Supreme Judicial Court, 72.)

The allowance of this whole line of cross-examination is severely criti-
cized by the *Yale Law Journal* in a detailed examination of the applicable
legal principles and authorities. The effect of what was done is thus summarized: "* * * the Commonwealth was allowed to ask, at a time of in-
tense popular feeling against anarchists and all opposed to the established
order, questions emphasizing in a picturesque and telling manner the political
views of a defendant on trial for a crime which admittedly had not the
slightest relation to those views." (36 *Yale Law Journal* 384, 388.)

Comparing this cross-examination to which Sacco was subjected with
the refusal to allow the defense to impeach the credibility of Goodridge by
proof of his admission of guilt of a crime for which, through the District
Attorney's intervention, he was given probation (see *supra*, p. 25), the *Yale
Law Journal* makes this comment: "Whatever may be the case in other
jurisdictions, Massachusetts can hardly justify giving the narrowest possible range to the shortest and simplest method of impeachment, a conviction, and the widest possible range to the most protracted and dangerous
method, cross-examination to an unconventional past." (36 *Yale Law
Journal* 384, 389–90.)

defendants by which their conduct was explained, the District Attorney adopted their confession of radicalism, exaggerated and exploited it. He thereby wholly destroyed the basis of his original claim, for what reason was there any longer to suppose that the "consciousness of guilt" was consciousness of murder rather than of radicalism?

CHAPTER IV

THE deliberate effort to excite the emotions of jurors still in the grip of war fever is not unparalleled in the legal history of the times. During the years 1918–19 in the United States, forty-four convictions were reversed by appellate courts for misconduct of the trial judge or the public prosecutor; thirty-three of them for inflammatory appeals made by the district attorney on matters not properly before the jury.[1] Appellate courts interfere reluctantly in such cases and only where there has been a flagrant abuse, so that we may safely assume that the above figures indicate an even more widespread evil. In a New York case[2] the district attorney urged on the jury that the name of the accused (Esposito) meant "bastard," and that he was an alien and within the draft age. The New York Court of Appeals set aside the conviction, and happily appellate courts in general have taken a firm stand against such practices.[3] What *is* unparalleled

---

[1] See 33 *Harvard Law Review* 956, and the comment of former Justice Charles E. Hughes: "And in the conduct of trials before the courts we find a growing tendency on the part of prosecutors to resort to grossly unfair practices." (Address at Centennial Celebration of Harvard Law School, June 21, 1920.)

[2] *People* v. *Esposito*, 224 N. Y. 370.

[3] See, for instance, the language of the Tennessee court in *Roland* v. *State*, 137 Tenn. 663, at 665 (1917): "It is the duty of the Court and counsel to be at special pains to see that race prejudice is entirely eliminated from the proceedings." And see the recent Kansas case of *State* v. *Powell*, 245 Pac. Rep. 128, 142.

is that such an abuse should have succeeded in a Massachusetts court.

As things were, what wonder the jury convicted? The last words left with them by Mr. Katzmann were an appeal to their solidarity against the alien: —

Gentlemen of the jury, do your duty. Do it like men. Stand together, you men of Norfolk! (R. 1135.)

The first words of Judge Thayer's charge revived their memories of the war and sharpened their indignation against the two draft-dodgers whose fate lay in their hands: —

The Commonwealth of Massachusetts called upon you to render a most important service. Although you knew that such service would be arduous, painful and tiresome, yet you, like the true soldier, responded to that call in the spirit of supreme American loyalty. There is no better word in the English language than "loyalty." (R. 1137.)

It had been to the accompaniment of this same war motif that the jurors were first initiated into the case; [1] by the license allowed to the prosecution it had been

[1] In addressing those who had been summoned to serve as jurors in the case Judge Thayer said: "It is not a sufficient excuse that a juror has business engagements and other duties more profitable and pleasant that he would rather perform, for you must remember the American soldier boy had other duties that he, too, would rather have performed than those that resulted in giving up his life on the battlefields of France, but he with undaunted courage and patriotic devotion that brought honor and glory to humanity and the world, rendered the service and made the supreme sacrifice. * * * I call upon you to render this service here that you have been summoned to perform, with the same spirit of patriotism, courage and devotion to duty as was exhibited by our soldier boy across the seas, * * * There is one thought which I would like to burn into the fibre of every citizen throughout this land, which is that he who is willing to accept the blessings of this Government should be perfectly willing to assume his share of its duties and responsibilities." (R. 16–17.)

dinned into their ears; and now by the final and authoritative voice of the Court it was a soldier's loyalty which was made the measure of their duty.

The function of a judge's charge is to enable the jury to find its way through the maze of conflicting testimony, to sift the relevant from the irrelevant, to weigh wisely, and to judge dispassionately. A trial judge is not expected to rehearse all the testimony; in Massachusetts he is not allowed to express his own opinion on it. But in drawing together the threads of evidence and marshaling the claims on both sides he must exercise a scrupulous regard for relevance and proportion. Misplaced emphasis here and omission there may work more damage than any outspoken comment. By his summing-up a judge reveals his estimate of relative importance. Judge Thayer's charge directs the emotions only too clearly. What guidance does he give to the mind? The charge occupies twenty-four pages. Of these, fourteen are consumed in abstract legal generalities and moral exhortations, paying lip service to the ideals of justice. Having allowed the minds of the jurors to be impregnated with war feeling, Judge Thayer now invited them to breathe "a purer atmosphere of unyielding impartiality and absolute fairness." (R. 1140.) Unfortunately the passion and prejudice systematically instilled during the course of a trial cannot be exorcised by the general, placid language of a charge after the mischief is done. Every experienced lawyer knows that it is idle to ask jurors to dismiss from their memory what has been deposited in their feelings.

In this case, surely the vital issue was identification. That the whole mass of conflicting identification testimony is dismissed in two pages out of twenty-four is a fair measure of the distorted perspective in which the Judge placed the case. He dealt with identification in abstract terms[1] and without mentioning the name of any witness on either side. The alibi testimony he likewise dismissed in two paragraphs, again without any reference to specific witnesses. In striking contrast to this sterile treatment of the issue whether or not Sacco and Vanzetti were in South Braintree on April 15 was his concrete and elaborate treatment of the inferences which might be drawn from the character of their conduct on the night of their arrest. Five pages of the charge are given over to "consciousness of guilt," set forth in great detail and with specific mention of the testimony given by the various police officials and by Mr. and Mrs. Johnson. The disproportionate consideration which Judge Thayer gave to

[1] On the part played by a court's charge and the qualities that should characterize it, see *People* v. *Odell*, 230 N. Y. 481, 487–8: "The court's charge is of supreme importance to the accused. It should be the safeguard of fairness and impartiality and the guarantee of judicial indifference to individuals. Defendant's case on its own facts was before the jury, not the case of the mere abstraction — 'a person charged with crime,' yet the charge is largely a statement of legal definitions of the degrees of felonious homicide, of reasonable doubt and the like, given abstractly and with little if any material reference to the evidence. The better practice for the court in a criminal case, emphatically in a capital case, even when uninvited by the defendant, is to present to the jury the case on trial in all the phases in which the jury ought to consider it. * * * The trial judge should not as a rule limit himself to stating good set terms of law culled from the codes and the reports. Jurors need not legal definitions merely. They require proper instructions as to the method of applying such definitions after reaching their conclusions on the facts."

this issue, in the light of his comments during the trial, must have left the impression on the jury that the case turned on "consciousness of guilt." As we have seen, Judge Thayer himself did in fact so interpret the jury's verdict afterward.

As to motive, the Court expatiated for more than a page on its legal conception and the undisputed claim of the Commonwealth that the motive of the murder of Parmenter and Berardelli was robbery, but made no comment whatever on the complete failure of the Commonwealth to trace any of the stolen money to either defendant or to connect them with the art of robbery. Undoubtedly, great weight must have been attached by the jury, as it was by the Court, to the identification of the fatal bullet taken from Berardelli's body as having passed through Sacco's pistol. This is a point soon to be dealt with in detail. Here the summary statement must suffice that the Court instructed the jury that Captain Proctor and another expert had testified in effect that "it was his [Sacco's] pistol that fired the bullet that caused the death of Berardelli" (R. 1152), when in fact, as we shall see, that was not Captain Proctor's testimony. Of course, if the jury believed Proctor's testimony as interpreted by Judge Thayer Sacco was doomed. In view of the temper of the times, the nature of the accusation, the opinions of the accused, the tactics of the prosecution, and the conduct of the Judge, no wonder the "men of Norfolk" convicted Sacco and Vanzetti!

Hitherto the prejudicial methods pursued by the

prosecution, which explain the convictions, rested on inferences, however compelling. But recently facts have been disclosed, and not denied by the prosecution, to show that the case against Sacco and Vanzetti for murder was part of a collusive effort between the District Attorney and agents of the Department of Justice to rid the country of these Italians because of their Red activities. In proof of this we have the affidavits of two former officers of the Government, one of whom served as post-office inspector for twenty-five years, and both of whom are now in honorable civil employment. The names of Sacco and Vanzetti were on the files of the Department of Justice "as radicals to be watched"; the Department was eager for their deportation, but had not evidence enough to secure it, and inasmuch as the United States District Court for Massachusetts had checked abuses in deportation proceedings [1] the Department had become chary of resorting to deportation without adequate legal basis. The arrest of Sacco and Vanzetti, on the mistaken theory of Stewart, furnished the agents of the Department of Justice their opportunity. Although the opinion of the agents working on the case was that "the South Braintree crime was the work of professionals" and that Sacco and Vanzetti "although anarchists and agitators, were not highway robbers, and had nothing to do with the South Braintree crime" (M. R. 146), yet they collaborated with the District Attorney in the prosecution of Sacco and Vanzetti for murder. For "it was the opinion of the Department

[1] *Colyer* v. *Keffington*, 256 Fed. 17.

agents here that a conviction of Sacco and Vanzetti for murder would be one way of disposing of these two men." (M. R. 146) Here, to be sure, is a startling allegation. But it is made by a man of long years of important service in the Government's employ; it is supported by the now admitted installation of a government spy in a cell adjoining Sacco's with a view to "obtaining whatever incriminating evidence he could * * * after winning his confidence" (M. R. 145), by the insinuation of an "under cover man" into the councils of the Sacco-Vanzetti Defense Committee, by the proposed placement of another spy as a lodger in Mrs. Sacco's house, and by the supplying of information about the radical activities of Sacco and Vanzetti to the District Attorney by the agents of the Department of Justice. These joint labors between Boston agents of the Department of Justice and the District Attorney led to a great deal of correspondence between the agent in charge and the District Attorney and to reports between the agents of the Department and Washington: —

There is, or was, a great deal of correspondence on file in the Boston office between Mr. West [the then agent in charge] and Mr. Katzmann, the District Attorney, and there are also copies of reports sent to Washington about the case. Letters and reports were made in triplicate; two copies were sent to Washington and one retained in Boston. The letters and documents on file in the Boston office would throw a great deal of light upon the preparation of the Sacco-Vanzetti case for trial, and upon the real opinion of the Boston office of the Department of Justice as to the guilt of Sacco and Vanzetti of the particular crime with which they were charged. (M. R. 146.)

These records have not been made available, nor
has their absence been accounted for. An appeal to
Attorney-General Sargent proved fruitless, although
supported by Senator Butler of Massachusetts, re-
questing that West "be authorized to talk with [counsel
for Sacco and Vanzetti] and to show me whatever
documents and correspondence are on file in his office
dealing with the investigations made by the Boston
agents before, during, and after the trial of Sacco and
Vanzetti." (M. R. 359.) The facts upon which this
appeal was made stand uncontradicted. West made
no denial whatever, and Katzmann only emphasized
his failure to deny the facts charged by the two former
agents of the Department of Justice by an affidavit
confined to a denial of some of the statements of a
former government spy. The charge that the principal
agent of the Department of Justice in Boston and the
District Attorney collaborated to secure the conviction
of Sacco and Vanzetti is denied neither by the agent
nor by the District Attorney. Instead, Stewart takes
it upon himself to say that the officials of the Department "had nothing whatsoever to do with the preparation of this case for trial." (M. R. 250.) Instead of
making a full disclosure of the facts, the representative
of the Commonwealth[1] indulged in vituperation against
the former officers of the Department of Justice as
men who were guilty of "a breach of loyalty" because
they violated the watchword of the Department of

---

[1] It has seemed best to depart from the chronological summary of the
successive stages of the case by quoting at this point from the arguments
and the decision upon the last motion for a new trial.

Justice "Do not betray the secrets of your departments." [1] To which Mr. Thompson rightly replied:
"What are the secrets which they admit? * * * A
government which has come to value its own secrets
more than it does the lives of its citizens has become a
tyranny. * * * Secrets, secrets! And he says you
should abstain from touching this verdict of your
jury because it is so sacred. Would they not have
liked to know something about the secrets? The case
is admitted by that inadvertent concession. There
are, then, secrets to be admitted." [2] Yet Judge Thayer

[1] From the argument of Assistant District Attorney Ranney in oppos-
ing the motion for a new trial, September 1926: "But what of Letherman
and Weyand? There is one outstanding thing to notice about both these
affidavits from the start. Your Honor knows the formation, the construc-
tion and the workings of the Department of Justice, that great department
centred in Washington with branches all over this country. That is the
police force, the police detective force, fundamentally, of the United States
government, without which we might have rebellion and revolution in this
country — a necessary arm of perhaps the greatest department in our
government. Your Honor knows that in all police departments, in all detective departments secrecy is a watchword, a byword — 'Do not betray
the secrets of your departments.' And if the secrets were broadcast, what
would be the result? There would be no crime detected and punished. And
yet Letherman and Weyand give their affidavits to these defendants and
betray the secrecy of their department. Talk of confidential files and cases
that have gone before! Now, we say on the face of it that there is a breach
of loyalty, and we wonder if we cannot conscientiously and logically find
that these men, not now in the department, did not leave there with honor
but with dishonor."

[2] From the argument in reply, by William G. Thompson: "I repel the
charge that Mr. Letherman, who is a man who was for twenty-five years
in the government service, one of the most respected employes that there
ever was in the Post Office Building, and who now holds an important
position in the Beacon Trust Company, and Mr. Weyand, who is now in
the Attorney General's office of the state of Maine — I repel the charge
that those men have done anything wrong in doing this, but on the contrary they have rendered one of the greatest public services that could be
rendered. What they have done is to point out and disclose the fact that

found in these circumstances only opportunity to make innuendo against a former official of the Government, well known for his long and honorable service. He indulged in much patriotic protestation, but is wholly silent about the specific acts of wrongdoing and lawlessness connected with the Red raids of 1920. The historian who relied on his opinion would assume that the charge of lawlessness and misconduct in the deportation of outlawed radicals was the traitorous invention of a diseased mind.

a condition of affairs, already made public before Judge Anderson, commented upon by the twelve lawyers to whom I called your Honor's attention, and common knowledge from one end of the country to the other, applied to this case as well as to many others. That is all they have done.

"In the language of Judge Hughes about this very matter, talking about disclosing and betraying secrets — here is Judge Hughes speaking about this in public: 'We cannot afford to ignore the indications that, perhaps to an extent unparalleled in our history, the essentials of liberty are being disregarded. Very recently information has been laid by responsible citizens at the bar of public opinion of violations of personal rights which savor of the worst practices of tyranny.'

"And it is charged here that two of these men who ventured, in the interest of life and liberty, to point out that those same practices were applied to these two men, that that office is full of documents tending to show the innocence of these two men and an improper combination, bargain, between the Department of Justice and the local District Attorney — it is charged here that those men have done something wrong. Is your Honor going to deal in secrets?"

CHAPTER V

THE verdict of guilty was brought in on July 14, 1921. The exceptions which had been taken to rulings at the trial were made the basis of an application for a new trial, which Judge Thayer refused. Subsequently a great mass of new evidence was unearthed by the defense, and made the subject of other motions for a new trial, all heard before Judge Thayer and all denied by him. The hearing on the later motions took place on October 1, 1923, and was the occasion of the entry into the case of Mr. William G. Thompson, a powerful advocate bred in the traditions of the Massachusetts courts. The espousal of the Sacco-Vanzetti cause by a man of Mr. Thompson's professional prestige at once gave it a new complexion and has been its mainstay ever since. For he has brought to the case not only his great ability as a lawyer, but the strength of his conviction that these two men are innocent and that their trial was not characterized by those high standards which are the pride of Massachusetts justice.

Some of the motions presented are technical in the extreme, and here no more can be attempted than to indicate their contents in the barest outline, reserving only one of them, the so-called Proctor motion, for more detailed treatment.

1. *Ripley motion.* The foreman of the jury, Ripley, a former chief of police of Quincy (who as such must

have carried great weight with his fellow jurors), after the conviction stated to the defense that he carried in his pocket at the trial cartridges of make and calibre similar to some of those put in evidence, and that there was discussion between him and other jurors about them. Presumably comparisons were made between Ripley's cartridges and the exhibits in the trial and inferences drawn therefrom. For whatever purpose they were used, the introduction of such "evidence" violated the conception of due process of law which insists that all evidence, particularly in a capital case, must be given openly in court so as to be put to the test of cross-examination.

2. *Daly motion.* Daly, an old friend of Ripley's, affirmed that he had, a few days before the trial opened, met Ripley at the railroad station. Ripley told him that he was going to serve on the jury in the case of the two "ginneys" charged with murder at Braintree, and upon his (Daly's) saying that he did not believe Sacco and Vanzetti were guilty Ripley replied, "Damn them, they ought to hang anyway." The unfitness of a man in this frame of mind to serve on a jury needs no comment.

3. *Hamilton motion.* Hamilton, an expert of fifteen years' experience in the microscopic examination of exhibits in criminal cases, who had been called in 165 homicide cases from Maine to Arizona, gave in the form of an affidavit the result of his examination under a compound microscope of the bullet taken from Berardelli's body and the revolver found on Vanzetti, supported by photographs taken under powerful mag-

nification. In his opinion minute comparison of the scratches on the bullet and the grooves inside the barrel of Sacco's pistol conclusively disproved the claim of the Commonwealth that it was from Sacco's pistol that the fatal bullet was fired.

4. *Gould motion.* Gould, who was in the business of selling razor paste to employees of factories, gave an affidavit to the following effect. He arrived in South Braintree on April 15, 1920, at about 3 P.M. and inquired where the shoe employees were paid off. Someone told him, "There goes the paymaster now; follow him," and he started to follow Parmenter and Berardelli down the street, when suddenly the shooting began. An automobile passed him within five feet; he saw a man with a revolver in his hand climb from the back to the front seat on the right-hand side of the driver and that man pointed a revolver at him and fired, the bullet passing through his overcoat. Gould had thus a better view of the man alleged to be Sacco than any witness on either side. He gave his name and address to the police, but was never called upon to testify. When, after the trial, Gould saw Sacco and Vanzetti, he was flat and unqualified in his statement that neither was the man he saw in the car. Judge Thayer's decision denying the Gould motion contains an extraordinary instance of his inaccuracy in matters of fact, which deserves quotation, not as unique, but as typical. By way of discrediting the affidavit he remarks that Gould did not see Sacco from April 15, 1920, until November 10, 1921, and yet was able to carry a correct picture of him in his mind all

this time — eighteen months. The whole burden of
Gould's affidavit was that the man he saw on April 15,
1920, was *not* Sacco, and therefore, far from carrying a
mental picture of Sacco in his mind for eighteen months,
he had never seen Sacco before he saw him in the jail.

5. *Proctor motion.* We have now reached a stage of
the case the details of which shake one's confidence in
the whole course of the proceedings and reveal a situation which in and of itself undermines the respect
usually to be accorded to a jury's verdict. By prearrangement the prosecution brought before the jury
a piece of evidence apparently most damaging to the
defendants, when in fact the *full* truth concerning this
evidence was very favorable to them. Vital to the
identification of Sacco and Vanzetti as the murderers
was the identification of one of the fatal bullets as a
bullet coming from Sacco's pistol. The evidence excluded the possibility that five other bullets found in
the dead bodies were fired either by Sacco or by Vanzetti. When Judge Thayer placed the case in the jury's
hands for judgment he charged them that the Commonwealth had introduced the testimony of two experts, Proctor and Van Amburgh, to the effect that
the fatal bullet went through Sacco's pistol. Such was
not the belief of Proctor; he refused to accede to this
view in the course of the preparation of the case, and
the District Attorney knew that such was not intended
to be his testimony. These startling statements call
for detailed proof.

Proctor at the time of his testimony was head of
the state police and had been in the Department of

Public Safety for twenty-three years. On the witness stand he was qualified at length as an expert who had for twenty years been making examination of and experiments with bullets and revolvers and had testified in over a hundred capital cases. His testimony was thus offered by the State as entitled to the greatest weight. If the jury could be convinced that the bullet found in Berardelli's body came out of Sacco's pistol, the State's case was invincible. On this crucial issue Captain Proctor testified as follows at the trial: —

Q. Have you an opinion as to whether bullet No. 3 [Exhibit 18] was fired from the Colt automatic, which is in evidence [Sacco's pistol]? A. I have.

Q. And what is your opinion? A. My opinion is that it is consistent with being fired from that pistol. (R. 472.)

The Government placed chief reliance on the expert testimony. In his closing argument the District Attorney told the jury: "You might disregard all the identification testimony, and base your verdict on the testimony of these experts." It weighed heavily in the Court's charge. In simple English Judge Thayer interpreted the evidence to mean that

it was his [Sacco's] pistol that fired the bullet that caused the death of Berardelli. To this effect the Commonwealth introduced the testimony of two witnesses, Messrs. Proctor and Van Amburgh. (R. 1152.)

Naturally the Court's interpretation became the jury's. By their silence, both the District Attorney and the counsel for the defense apparently acquiesced in the Court's interpretation. After the conviction

Proctor in an affidavit swore to the following account of his true views and the manner in which they were phrased for purposes of the trial. After giving his experience and stating the fact that he had had the custody of the bullets, cartridges, shells, and pistols in the case, he swore that one of the bullets

was, as I then testified and still believe, fired from *a* Colt automatic pistol of 32 calibre. During the preparation for the trial, my attention was repeatedly called by the District Attorney and his assistants to the question: whether I could find any evidence which would justify the opinion that the particular bullet taken from the body of Berardelli, which came from *a* Colt automatic pistol, came from the particular Colt automatic pistol taken from Sacco. I used every means available to me for forming an opinion on this subject. I conducted, with Captain Van Amburgh, certain tests at Lowell, about which I testified, consisting in firing certain cartridges through Sacco's pistol. At no time was I able to find any evidence whatever which tended to convince me that the particular model bullet found in Berardelli's body, which came from *a* Colt automatic pistol, which I think was numbered 3 and had some other exhibit number, came from Sacco's pistol, and I so informed the District Attorney and his assistant before the trial. This bullet was what is commonly called a full metalpatch bullet and although I repeatedly talked over with Captain Van Amburgh the scratch or scratches which he claimed tended to identify this bullet as one that must have gone through Sacco's pistol, his statements concerning the identifying marks seemed to me entirely unconvincing.

At the trial, the District Attorney did not ask me whether I had found any evidence that the so-called mortal bullet which I have referred to as number 3 passed through Sacco's pistol, nor was I asked that question on cross-examination. The District Attorney desired to ask me that question, but I had *repeatedly* told him that if he did I should be obliged to answer

in the negative; consequently, he put to me this question:
Q. Have you an opinion as to whether bullet number 3 was
fired from the Colt automatic which is in evidence? To which
I answered, "I have." He then proceeded. Q. And what is
your opinion? A. My opinion is that it is consistent with being
fired by that pistol. (Brief for Defendants on· first appeal
before Supreme Judicial Court, 161.) [Italics ours.]

He proceeded to state that he is still of the same
opinion,

but I do not intend by that answer to imply that I had found
any evidence that the so-called mortal bullet had passed through
this particular Colt automatic pistol and the District Attorney
well knew that I did not so intend and framed his question accordingly. Had I been asked the direct question: whether I
had found any affirmative evidence whatever that this so-called
mortal bullet had passed through this particular Sacco's pistol,
I should have answered then, as I do now without hesitation,
in the negative. (Brief for Defendants on first appeal before
Supreme Judicial Court, 161.)

This affidavit of Proctor's was made the basis of
Mr. Thompson's motion for a new trial before Judge
Thayer. Here was a charge going to the vitals of the
case, made by a high official of the police agencies of
the state. How did the District Attorney meet it?
Mr. Katzmann and his assistant, Mr. Williams, filed
affidavits in reply. Did they contradict Proctor?
They could not deny his testimony or the weight that
the prosecution and the Court had attached to it.
These were matters of record. Did they deny the
prearrangement which he charged? Did they deny
that he told them he was unable to identify the mortal
bullet as Sacco's bullet? Let their affidavits speak.

Katzmann stated that,

prior to his testifying, Captain Proctor told me that he was prepared to testify that the mortal bullet was consistent with having been fired from the Sacco pistol; that I did not *repeatedly* ask him whether he had found any evidence that the mortal bullet had passed through the Sacco pistol, nor did he *repeatedly* tell me that if I did ask him that question he would be obliged to reply in the negative. (Supplementary Bill of Exceptions, 147.) [Italics ours.]

Williams's affidavit, after setting forth that Captain Proctor told him before the trial that comparisons of the mortal bullet with bullets "pushed by him through various types of pistols" showed that "the mortal bullet had been fired in *a* Colt automatic pistol," proceeded: —

He [Proctor] said that all he could do was to determine the width of the landmarks upon the bullet. His attention was not repeatedly called to the question, whether he could find any evidence which would justify the opinion that this bullet came from the Sacco pistol. I conducted the direct examination of Captain Proctor at the trial and asked him the question quoted in his affidavit, "Have you an opinion as to whether bullet number 3 was fired from the Colt automatic which is in evidence?"

This question was suggested by Captain Proctor himself as best calculated to give him an opportunity to tell what opinion he had respecting the mortal bullet and its connection with the Sacco pistol. His answer in court was the same answer he had given me personally before. (Supplementary Bill of Exceptions, 148.)

Proctor's disclosures remain uncontradicted: he was unable to identify the murder bullet as Sacco's bullet; he told Katzmann and Williams that he was unable to do it; he told them that if he were asked the question on the witness stand he would have to testify that he could not make the identification; a form of words was therefore found by which, without committing perjury, he could convey the impression that he had testified to the identification. The only contradiction by Katzmann and Williams of Proctor's account affects the number of times that he told them that he was unable to make the identification, he having sworn that he told them "repeatedly" and they denying that he told them "repeatedly." Can there be any dissent among impartial minds from the way in which Mr. Thompson characterized this transaction in his argument before Judge Thayer: —

> In your closing charge, your honor, you disclosed the importance which you attached to the testimony of these experts. The former District Attorney and the present District Attorney do not deny that the jury got an erroneous understanding, and that your honor got an erroneous understanding of the testimony of one of these witnesses. They heard your honor's charge. Did they rise in their seats to correct you? No, they sat by and said never a word. They profited by Captain Proctor's testimony. How can that be reconciled with a desire to be fair to men on trial for their lives? The more I reflect upon this matter, the worse it grows.[1]

Yet Judge Thayer found no warrant in the Proctor incident for directing a new trial. And why?

1. The Judge quotes the Proctor questions and answers and argues that the questions were clear and must have been perfectly understood by Captain

[1] From the stenographic minutes of Mr. Thompson's argument on the Proctor motion.

Proctor. Of course, the questions were clear and clearly understood by Proctor. The whole meaning of Captain Proctor's affidavit was that the questions and answers were prearranged and that by this pre-arrangement Court and jury were misled with terrible harm to the defendants.

2. Judge Thayer then inquires whether there was anything "unfair or improper" in the questions put by the District Attorney and whether they did not "invite Captain Proctor to state his true opinion at that time." Here again the entire point of Proctor's affidavit was perverted. The questions and answers are significant, not in themselves, but because of the prearrangement to ask and to answer them. The issue is the propriety of this prearrangement between the District Attorney and Captain Proctor and the effect of this prearrangement upon the jury's mind.

3. The Judge next asks why Captain Proctor did not, in answer to the question put to him, say that he had found no "affirmative evidence whatever that this so-called mortal bullet had passed through this particular Sacco's pistol." This is another amazing twist of the meaning of the Proctor affidavit. Captain Proctor swore that by prearrangement with the District Attorney the direct question whether he had found such evidence was avoided and a question formulated which would enable him to mislead the jury as it misled the Court. If the "direct question" had been put to him he would, as he says, have been obliged to answer in the negative and thereby, of course, would have disastrously affected the Commonwealth's case.

4. The Judge is extraordinarily versatile in misinterpreting the true purport of the Proctor affidavit. Thus, he seriously asks why, if Captain Proctor at the trial was "desirous of expressing his true opinion," he used the phrase "consistent with," language selected by himself. The crux of the Proctor motion was that Captain Proctor at the trial was not "desirous of expressing his true opinion," that the District Attorney was very desirous that he should not do so, and that between them they agreed on a form of words to avoid it.

5. Judge Thayer thus indicates the real question in issue: —

> I am asked to believe that when Captain Proctor testified in court to the effect that when he said it was consistent with being fired through the Sacco pistol, he intended to mean that it might have been fired through any .32 calibre Colt automatic, and that was all.   (Supplementary Bill of Exceptions, 167.)

The affidavits of Proctor, Katzmann, and Williams leave no doubt of what was intended. It was arranged that the jury should understand that Proctor meant that in his opinion the bullet had passed through Sacco's pistol. Proctor knew and the District Attorney knew, but they did not intend the jury to know, that he had found no evidence in support of that opinion.

6. The Court then proceeds to charge Mr. Thompson with this argument on the strength of the Proctor incident: —

> That the District Attorney, knowing that Captain Proctor honestly believed that the mortal bullet was not fired through the Sacco pistol, by prearrangement with Captain Proctor

prevailed on him to compromise the truth, in that Captain Proctor should testify that it was his opinion that it was consistent with its having been fired through the Sacco pistol. In other words, that Captain Proctor, by prearrangement (which means intentional) compromised the truth with the District Attorney by his (Captain Proctor's) testifying knowingly to something that was false. (Supplementary Bill of Exceptions, 167.)

Here again the Court tortures the Proctor material out of shape. No one suggested that Captain Proctor "honestly believed that the mortal bullet was not fired through the Sacco pistol." What he says he believed, and what nobody denies he believed, was that there was no evidence whatever to show it was fired through that pistol and not some other Colt automatic pistol of the same calibre. Nor did Mr. Thompson contend that Proctor testified "knowingly to something that was false." A more subtle mischief was involved in the prearrangement between the District Attorney and Proctor. Proctor used language which was true in one sense but false in the meaning it conveyed to those not privy to the arrangement. It was hoped that it would be understood in the false sense and it *was* understood in the false sense by the Judge himself in charging the jury. Formal accuracy was consciously resorted to as a means of misleading the Court and jury.

7. The Judge next tries to belittle the significance of the Proctor incident by seeking to reduce Proctor's qualifications and authority as an expert, two years after he was offered by the Commonwealth with elaborate reliance as a most important expert. We cannot go into the details of numerous misstatements of in-

controvertible fact by which the Judge thus seeks to escape the harm that Proctor wrought on the jury's mind. We must dwell, however, on one amazing statement of the Court. "With his limited knowledge," says Judge Thayer,

Captain Proctor did not testify that the mortal bullet did pass through Sacco's pistol, but that from his examination of the facts it was simply consistent with it. (Supplementary Bill of Exceptions, 168.)

Why did not Judge Thayer say this to the jury when he charged them with determining the guilt or innocence of Sacco, instead of discovering that it is what Captain Proctor testified, more than three years after the verdict of the jury found him guilty? Why did the Judge charge the jury that Captain Proctor *did* testify that the mortal bullet passed through Sacco's pistol? And why, having in October 1924, for the purpose of denying the Proctor motion, minimized the Proctor testimony by saying that Proctor testified that the passing of the mortal bullet through Sacco's pistol was "simply consistent with" the facts, does he two years later, in order to show how strong the case was at the original trial, state that the "experts testified in their judgment it [the mortal bullet] was *perfectly* consistent with" having been fired through the Sacco pistol? In his charge Judge Thayer misled the jury by maximizing the Proctor testimony as the prearrangement intended that it should be maximized. When the prearrangement was discovered and made the basis of a motion for a new trial, Judge Thayer depreciated Proctor's qualifications as an expert and minimized

Proctor's actual testimony. Finally, when confronted with new evidence pointing not only away from Sacco and Vanzetti but positively in another direction, in order to give the appearance of impressiveness to the facts before the jury, Judge Thayer again relies upon the weightiness of Proctor's expert testimony and maximizes his evidence at the trial, but not to the extent that he did in charging the jury, because Proctor's affidavit now prevents him from so doing.

8. The battledore-and-shuttlecock method is further illustrated by the Court's treatment of his own understanding of Captain Proctor's testimony at the trial as indicated by his charge: —

It is not the duty of the Court, in charging a jury, to deal with the weight and probative effect of testimony of witnesses. (Supplementary Bill of Exceptions, 168.)

True! But the Court assumed it to be his duty to state the testimony and that is what Judge Thayer undertook to do in this case. Presumably the Court stated to the jury the effect of Captain Proctor's testimony as he understood it at the time and as it was intended by Captain Proctor and the District Attorney that it should be understood. Certainly the jury could have been in no possible doubt as to how Captain Proctor's testimony lay in Judge Thayer's mind.[1]

[1] The following from a recent New York case is pertinent: "The determination that he was guilty depends upon inferences which the jury might doubtless draw. But errors or omissions which had the case been clearer might have been overlooked, here assume great importance. The jury was entitled in its difficult task to every aid which the court could give it. We must see that it was not misled." (*People* v. *Montesanto*, 236 N. Y. 396, 405 (1923).)

9. Finally, Judge Thayer characterized the affidavits of Katzmann and Williams as "clear and convincing"; but not a word as to what is made clear by them and of what they convinced the reader. He concludes by saying that he "never observed anything" on the part of Katzmann and Williams "but what was consistent with the highest standard of professional conduct."

This is the attitude of mind which has guided the conduct of this case from the beginning; this is the judge who has, for all practical purposes, sat in judgment upon his own conduct. Having heard Proctor testify at the trial that the fatal bullet was "consistent with having gone through" Sacco's pistol, he charged the jury that Proctor had in effect testified it did go through. Having read the uncontradicted affidavit of Proctor that he could not have testified, and did not mean to testify, that the mortal bullet was Sacco's, he denies the motion for retrial, partly because the questions that were put to Proctor and the answers that were given were unequivocal. Having decided that the Proctor incident was unimportant, two years later in reviewing the whole case he nevertheless changes his own interpretation of the testimony of Proctor from the damaging form in which he gave it to the jury. Even now, however, instead of quoting the language of Proctor, that the fatal bullet "was consistent with being fired through the Sacco pistol," Judge Thayer gives the testimony as "*perfectly* consistent."

English criminal justice is constantly held up to us, and rightly so, as an example. One ventures confidently to say that conduct like that revealed by the Proctor incident is inconceivable in an English prosecution. But if it did take place, there is no possible doubt that the corrective resources of the English courts would not allow a verdict secured by such means, especially in a capital case, to stand. Such behavior, uncorrected by the Court, surely violates the standards which the Massachusetts Supreme Judicial Court has laid down for district attorneys: —

The powers of a district attorney under our laws are very extensive. They affect to a high degree the liberty of the individual, the good order of society, and the safety of the community. His natural influence with the grand jury, and the confidence commonly reposed in his recommendations by judges, afford to the unscrupulous, the weak or the wicked incumbent of the office vast opportunity to oppress the innocent and to shield the guilty, to trouble his enemies and to protect his friends, and to make the interest of the public subservient to his personal desires, his individual ambitions and his private advantage. * * * Powers so great impose responsibilities correspondingly grave. They demand character incorruptible, reputation unsullied, a high standard of professional ethics, and sound judgment of no mean order.[1]

If the Proctor situation does not come within the condemnation of these requirements,[2] language certainly has strange meaning. Yet the Massachusetts Supreme

[1] *Attorney General* v. *Tufts*, 239 Mass. 458, 489 (1921).

[2] Pertinent to this and other phases of the case is Canon 5 of the Canons of Professional Ethics adopted by the American Bar Association: "The primary duty of a lawyer engaged in public prosecution is not to convict, but to see that justice is done. The suppression of facts or the secreting of witnesses capable of establishing the innocence of the accused is highly reprehensible." (51 Reports of American Bar Association 898, 899 (1926).)

Judicial Court held that Judge Thayer's decision could not "as a matter of law" be reversed.

In an opinion of sixty pages handed down on May 12, 1926, the Supreme Judicial Court of Massachusetts found "no error" in any of the rulings of Judge Thayer, and so the verdicts were allowed to stand.[1] It is important to realize what issues were argued before the Court and decided by it, and what issues were not presented to the Court or passed upon because outside the scope of its authority. A distinction familiar to every lawyer must be emphasized because Judge Thayer has since misconstrued what the Court did. The guilt or innocence of the defendants was not retried in the Supreme Judicial Court. That Court could not even inquire whether the facts as set forth in the printed record justified the verdict. Such would have been the scope of judicial review had the case come up before the New York Court of Appeals or the English Court of Criminal Appeal. In those jurisdictions a judgment upon the facts as well as upon the law is open, and their courts decide whether convictions should stand in view of the whole record. A much more limited scope in reviewing convictions prevails in Massachusetts. What is reviewed, in effect, is the conduct of the trial judge; only so-called questions of law are open. For instance, it was a question of law, and therefore subject to review by the Supreme Judicial Court, whether evidence should be admitted to prove that at the time Goodridge was testifying on behalf of the Commonwealth

[1] 255 Mass. 369.

the District Attorney let him go unpunished in a case of larceny to which he'had pleaded guilty; whether any inference of self-interest discrediting Goodridge's testimony of identification should be drawn would be a question of fact for the jury, and so outside the Supreme Court's power to review.

The merits of the legal questions raised by the Goodridge and other exceptions cannot be discussed here. Suffice it to say, with all deference, that some of the Supreme Judicial Court rulings are puzzling in the extreme. One question of law, however, can be explained within small compass, and that is the question which is the crux of the case: Did Judge Thayer observe the standards of Anglo-American justice? In legal parlance, was there "abuse of judicial discretion" by Judge Thayer? This is the theme which permeates the whole opinion of the Court. Recurring again and again we find such phrases as "this ruling also was within the discretionary power of the Court," "no abuse of discretion is shown." What, then, is "judicial discretion"? Is it a technical conception? Is it a legal abracadabra, or does it imply standards of conduct within the comprehension of the laity in whose interests they are enforced? The present Chief Justice of Massachusetts has given an authoritative definition: —

Discretion in this connection means a sound judicial discretion, enlightened by intelligence and learning, controlled by sound principles of law, of firm courage combined with the calmness of a cool mind, free from partiality, not swayed by sympathy nor warped by prejudice nor moved by any kind of influence save alone the overwhelming passion to do that which is just. It may be assumed that conduct manifesting abuse of judicial discretion will be reviewed and some relief afforded.[1]

This is the test by which Judge Thayer's conduct must be measured. The Supreme Judicial Court found no abuse of judicial discretion on the record presented at the first hearing before it. In other words, the Court was satisfied that throughout the conduct of the trial and the proceedings that followed it Judge Thayer was governed by "the calmness of a cool mind, free from partiality, not swayed by sympathy nor warped by prejudice nor moved by any kind of influence save alone the overwhelming passion to do that which is just."

The reader has now had placed before him fairly, it is hoped, however briefly, the means of forming a judgment. Let him judge for himself!

[1] *Davis* v. *Boston Elevated Ry.*, 235 Mass. 482, 496–7.

CHAPTER VI

HITHERTO the defense has maintained that the circumstances of the case all pointed away from Sacco and Vanzetti. But the deaths of Parmenter and Berardelli remained unexplained. Now the defense has adduced new proof, not only that Sacco and Vanzetti did *not* commit the murders, but also, positively, that a well-known gang of professional criminals *did* commit them. Hitherto a new trial has been pressed because of the character of the original trial. Now a new trial has been demanded because an impressive body of evidence tends to establish the guilt of others.

Celestino F. Madeiros, a young Portuguese with a bad criminal record, was in 1925 confined in the same prison with Sacco. On November 18, while his appeal from a conviction of murder committed in an attempt at bank robbery was pending in the Supreme Court, he sent to Sacco through a jail messenger the following note: —

I hear by confess to being in the South Braintree shoe company crime and Sacco and Vanzetti was not in said crime.

CELESTINO F. MADEIROS

The confession of a criminal assuming guilt for a crime laid at another's door is always suspect, and rightly so. But, as we cannot too strongly insist, the new evidence is not *contained in* the Madeiros confession. His note to Sacco was only the starting point which enabled the defense to draw the network of independent evidence around the Morelli gang of Providence.

As soon as Sacco's counsel was apprized of this note he began a searching investigation of Madeiros's claim. It then appeared that Madeiros had tried several times previously to tell Sacco that he knew the real perpetrators of the Braintree job, but Sacco, fearing he was a spy who tried to ensnare him, as Sacco well might, had disregarded what he said. An interview with Madeiros revealed such circumstantiality of detail that his examination, both by the defense and the Commonwealth, was plainly called for. Several affidavits given by Madeiros and a deposition of one hundred pages, in which he was cross-examined by the District Attorney, tell the following story.

In 1920 Madeiros, then eighteen years old, was living in Providence. He already had a criminal record and was associated with a gang of Italians engaged in robbing freight cars. One evening, when they were talking together in a saloon in Providence, some members of the gang invited him to join them in a pay-roll robbery at South Braintree. A holdup was a new form of criminal enterprise for him, but they told him "they had done lots of jobs of this kind" and persuaded him to come along. As an eighteen-year-old novice he was to be given only a subordinate part. He was to sit in the back of a car with a revolver and "help hold back the crowd in case they made a rush." Accordingly a few days later, on April 15, 1920, the plan was carried into execution. In the party, besides Madeiros, were three Italians and a "kind of a slim fellow with light hair," who drove the car. In order to prevent identification they adopted the familiar device of using two cars. They started out in a Hudson, driving to some woods near Randolph. They then exchanged the Hudson for a Buick brought them by another member of the gang. In the Buick they proceeded to South Braintree, arriving there about noon. When the time came the actual shooting was done by the oldest of the Italians, a man about forty, and one other. The rest of the party remained near by in the automobile. As the crime was being committed they drove up, took aboard the murderers and the money, and made off. They drove back to the Randolph woods, exchanged the Buick again for the Hudson, and returned to Providence. The arrangement was that Madeiros should meet the others in a saloon at Providence the following night to divide the spoils. Whether this arrangement was kept and whether he got any of the Braintree loot Madeiros persistently refused to say.

This refusal was in pursuance of Madeiros's avowed policy. From the outset he announced his determination not to reveal the identity of his associates in the Braintree job, while holding nothing back which seemed to implicate himself alone. To shield them he obstinately declined to answer questions and, if necessary, frankly resorted to lies. Thus, examination could not extort from him the surnames of the gang, and he further sought to cover up their identity by giving some of them false Christian names. He showed considerable astuteness in evading what he wanted to conceal. But in undertaking to tell the story of the crime without revealing the criminals he set himself an impossible task. In spite of his efforts, a lawyer as resourceful as Mr. Thompson was able to elicit facts which, when followed up, established the identity of the gang and also strongly corroborated the story of Madeiros.

Madeiros said that the gang "had been engaged in robbing freight cars in Providence." Was there such a gang whose composition and activities verified Madeiros's story and at the same time explained the facts of the Braintree crime? There was the Morelli gang, well known to the police of Providence and New Bedford as professional criminals, several of whom at the time of the Braintree murders were actually under indictment in the United States District Court of Rhode Island for stealing from freight cars. Five out of nine indictments charging shoe thefts were for stealing consignments from *Slater and Morrill at South Braintree* and from Rice and Hutchins, the factory next door. In view of their method of operations, the gang must have had a confederate at Braintree to spot shipments for them. The Slater and Morrill factory was about one hundred yards from the South Braintree railroad station and an accomplice spotting shipments would be passed by the paymaster on his weekly trip. It will be recalled that the pay roll was that of the Slater and Morrill factory and that the murders and the robbery occurred in front of the Slater and Morrill and Rice and Hutchins factories. The Morellis under indictment were out of jail awaiting trial. They needed money for their defense; their only source of income was crime. They were at large until May 25, when they were convicted and sent to Atlanta.

Madeiros did not name the gang, but described the men who were with him at Braintree. How did his descriptions fit the Morelli gang? The leader of the gang was Joe, aged thirty-nine. His brothers were Mike, Patsy, Butsy, and Fred. Other members were Bibba Barone, Gyp the Blood, Mancini, and Steve the Pole. Bibba Barone and Fred Morelli were in jail on April 15, 1920. According to Madeiros there were five, including himself, in the murder car, three of whom were Italians, and the driver "Polish or Finland or something northern Europe." The shooting was done by the oldest of the Italians, a man of about forty and another called Bill. A fourth Italian brought up the Buick car for exchange at Randolph. As far as his descriptions carry, Madeiros's party fits the members of the Morelli gang. But the testimony of independent witnesses corroborates Madeiros and makes the identification decisive. One of the gravest difficulties of the prosecution's case against Sacco and Vanzetti was the collapse of the Government's attempt to identify the driver of the murder car as Vanzetti. It will be recalled that the District Attorney told the jury that "they must be overwhelmed with the testimony that when the car started it was driven by a light-haired man, who gave every appearance of being sickly." Steve the Pole satisfies Madeiros's description of the driver as well as the testimony at the trial.

To set the matter beyond a doubt two women who were working in the Slater and Morrill factory identified Steve the Pole as the man they saw standing for half an hour by a car outside their window on that day. Two witnesses who testified at the trial identified Joe Morelli as one of the men who did the shooting and another identified Mancini. The Morellis were American-born, which explains the testimony at the trial that one of the bandits spoke clear and unmistakable English, a thing impossible to Sacco and Vanzetti.

Plainly the personnel of the Morelli gang fits the Braintree crime. What of other details? The mortal bullet came out of a 32 Colt; Joe Morelli had a 32 Colt at this time; Mancini's pistol was of a type and calibre to account for the other five bullets found in the victims. The "murder car" at the trial was a Buick. Madeiros said a Buick was used; and Mike Morelli, according to the New Bedford police, at this time was driving a Buick, which disappeared immediately after April 15, 1920. In fact, the police of New Bedford, where the Morelli gang had been operating, suspected them of the Braintree crime, but dropped the matter after the arrest of Sacco and Vanzetti. Shortly after the Braintree job, Madeiros was sent away for five months for larceny of an amount less than $100. But immediately after his release, he had about $2800 in bank, which enabled him to go on a pleasure trip to the West and Mexico. The $2800 is adequately accounted for only as his share of the Braintree booty: the loot was $15,776.51, and according to his story there were six men in the job. Joe Morelli,

we know, was sent to Atlanta for his share in the robbery of the Slater and Morrill shoes. While confined
he made an arrangement with a fellow prisoner whereby
the latter was to furnish him with an alibi if he ever
needed it, placing Morelli in New York on April 15,
1920.[1]

Even so compressed a précis of the evidence of many
witnesses will have made it clear that the defense has
built up a powerful case, without the resources at the
command of the State in criminal investigations. The
witnesses other than Madeiros of themselves afford
strong probability of the guilt of the Morellis. What
of the intrinsic credibility of Madeiros's confession,
which, if believed, settles the matter? A man who
seeks to relieve another of guilt while himself about to
undergo the penalty of death does not carry conviction.
The circumstances of Madeiros's confession, however,
free it from the usual suspicion and furnish assurances
of its trustworthiness. Far from having nothing to
lose by making the confession, Madeiros stood to
jeopardize his life. For while, to be sure, at the time
of his confession he was under sentence for another
murder, an appeal from this conviction was pending,
which was in fact successful in getting him a new trial.
Could anything be more prejudicial to an effort to reverse his conviction for one crime than to admit guilt for
another? So clearly prejudicial in fact was his confession
that by arrangement with the District Attorney it was
kept secret until after the outcome of his appeal and the
new trial which followed it. Moreover, the note of

[1] Carpenter Affidavit, Bill of Exceptions on Motion for New Trial, 108.

confession sent by Madeiros to Sacco on November
18 was not, as we have seen, his first communication
to Sacco. Nor was it his first explicit confession. The
murder for which he had been convicted, together
with a man named Weeks, — the Wrentham bank
crime, — was a holdup like the Braintree job. Weeks,
under life sentence in another jail, when questioned,
revealed that in planning the Wrentham job Madeiros
drew on his experience at Braintree. During their
partnership Madeiros, he said, frequently referred to the
Braintree job (M. R. 41), saying it was arranged by the
Morelli gang (whom Weeks knew), and at one time
identifying a speak-easy in which they found themselves as the one the gang visited before the Braintree
holdup. In planning the Wrentham job Madeiros
further told Weeks that he "had had enough of the
Buick in the South Braintree job." Before the Wrentham crime he had talked to the couple who kept the
roadhouse where for a time he was a "bouncer" of
his part in the Braintree crime, and said "that he would
like to save Sacco and Vanzetti because he knew they
were perfectly innocent."

These earlier disclosures by Madeiros refute the
theory that he was led to make his latest confession
by the hope of money. It is suggested that in November 1925 he had seen the financial statement of the
Sacco-Vanzetti Defense Committee. But the State
conceded that there was no evidence that "aid of
any description had been promised to Madeiros" on
behalf of the defendants. (M. R. 16.) Secondly, he
could not have had knowledge of this statement before

he talked to Weeks and the others, and when he attempted the prior communications to Sacco, because it was not then in existence. It is incredible that a man fighting for his life on a charge for one murder would, in the hope of getting money, falsely accuse himself of another murder. He knew the danger of a confession, for his conviction in the Wrentham case largely rested upon confessions made by him. Why should he be believed and suffer death when he confesses one crime and not be believed when he confesses another of the same character? Is not his own statement in accordance with the motives even of a murderer?

I seen Sacco's wife come up here [jail] with the kids and I felt sorry for the kids. (M. R. 303.)

In the light of all the information now available, which is the more probable truth: that Sacco and Vanzetti or the Morelli gang were the perpetrators of the Braintree murders? The Morelli theory accounts for all members of the Braintree murder gang; the Sacco-Vanzetti theory for only two, for it is conceded that if Madeiros was there, Sacco and Vanzetti were not. The Morelli theory accounts for all the bullets found in the dead men; the Sacco-Vanzetti theory for only one out of six. The Morelli explanation settles the motive, for the Morelli gang were criminals desperately in need of money for legal expenses pending their trial for felonies, whereas the Sacco-Vanzetti theory is unsupported by any motive. Moreover Madeiros's possession of $2800 accounts for his share of the booty, whereas not a penny has ever been traced to anybody or accounted for on the Sacco-Vanzetti theory. The Morelli story is not subject to the absurd premise that professional holdup men who stole automobiles at will and who had recently made a haul of nearly $16,000 would devote an evening, as did Sacco and Vanzetti the night of their arrest, to riding around on suburban street cars to borrow a friend's six-year-old Overland. The character of the Morelli gang fits the opinion of police investigators and the inherent facts of the situation, which tended to prove that the crime was the work of professionals, whereas the past character and record of Sacco and Vanzetti have always made it incredible that they should spontaneously become perpetrators of a bold murder, executed with the utmost expertness. A good worker regularly employed at his trade but away on a particular day which is clearly accounted for, and a dreamy fish peddler, openly engaged in political propaganda, neither do nor can suddenly commit an isolated job of highly professional banditry.[1]

Can the situation be put more conservatively than this? Every reasonable probability points away from Sacco and Vanzetti; every reasonable probability points toward the Morelli gang.

Surely, no jury of disinterested and informed lawyers would hesitate for a moment to hold that, if the evidence concerning the Braintree crime and the Morelli gang came before a magistrate, he would be bound to commit for the action of a grand jury; that a grand jury would clearly be justified in presenting a true

[1] See Appendix A.

bill against them; and that on trial a judge would submit such facts for a jury's verdict. The jury that tried and convicted Sacco and Vanzetti had no such facts before it; a jury trying them would in every likelihood find in the new facts controlling considerations for ascertaining the guilt or innocence of Sacco and Vanzetti.

How did these facts appear to Judge Thayer?

CHAPTER VII

At the outset, the scope of Judge Thayer's duty toward the motion for a new trial based upon this new evidence must be kept in mind. It was not for him to determine the guilt of the Morellis or the innocence of Sacco and Vanzetti; it was not for him to weigh the new evidence as though he were a jury, determining what is true and what is false. Judge Thayer's duty was the very narrow one of ascertaining whether here was new material fit for a new jury's judgment. May honest minds, capable of dealing with evidence, reach a different conclusion, because of the new evidence, from that of the first jury? Do the new facts raise debatable issues? Could another jury, conscious of its oath and conscientiously obedient to it, reach a verdict contrary to the one that was reached on a record wholly different from the present, in view of evidence recently discovered and not adducible by the defense at the time of the original trial? To all these questions Judge Thayer says, "No." This amazing conclusion he reached after studying the motion "for several weeks without interruption," and set forth in an opinion of 25,000 words! One can wish for nothing more than that every reader who has proceeded thus far should study the full text of this latest Thayer opinion. Space precludes its detailed treatment here. To quote it, to analyze it, adequately to comment upon it would require a volume in itself. Having now put the materials for detailed judgment at the disposal of readers, space permits only a few summary observations.

By what is left out and by what is put in, the uninformed reader of Judge Thayer's opinion would be wholly misled as to the real facts of the case. Speaking from a considerable experience as a prosecuting officer, whose special task for a time it was to sustain on appeal convictions for the Government, and whose scientific duties since have led to the examination of a great number of records and the opinions based thereon, I assert with deep regret, but without the slightest fear of disproof, that certainly in modern times Judge Thayer's opinion stands unmatched, happily, for discrepancies between what the record discloses and what the opinion conveys. His 25,000-word document cannot accurately be described otherwise than as a farrago of misquotations, misrepresentations, suppressions, and mutilations. The disinterested inquirer could not possibly derive from it a true knowledge of the new evidence that was submitted to him as the basis for a new trial. The opinion is literally honeycombed with demonstrable errors, and infused by a spirit alien to judicial utterance. A study of the opinion in the light of the record led the conservative *Boston Herald*, which long held the view that the sentence against these men should be carried out, to a frank reversal of its position: —

As months have merged into years and the great debate over this case has continued, our doubts have solidified slowly into convictions, and reluctantly we have found ourselves compelled to reverse our original judgment. We hope the Supreme Judicial Court will grant a new trial on the basis of the new evidence not yet examined in open court. * * * We have read the full decision in which Judge Webster Thayer, who presided at the original trial, renders his decision against the application for a new trial, and we submit that it carries the tone of the advocate rather than the arbitrator.[1]

Commenting on the restraint of the *Herald's* characterization of Judge Thayer's opinion, Dr. Morton Prince writes that any expert psychologist reading the Thayer opinion "could not fail to find evidences that portray strong personal feeling, poorly concealed, that should have no place in a judicial document." One or two illustrations must suffice. Mr. William G. Thompson is one of the leaders of the Boston bar. He has brought to the defense of these men the vigor of mind and the force of character which have given him his commanding position in the profession. Judge Thayer, however, thus characterized Mr. Thompson's activities in behalf of these two Italians: —

Since the trial before the Jury of these cases, a new type of disease would seem to have developed. It might be called "lego-psychic neurosis" or hysteria which means: "a belief in the existence of something which in fact and truth has no such existence." (M. R. 388.)

And this from a judge who gives meretricious authority to his self-justification by speaking of the verdict which convicted these men as "approved by the Supreme Judicial Court of this Commonwealth"! The

[1] See Appendix B for full text of *Boston Herald* editorial.

Supreme Court never approved the verdict; nor did it pretend to do so. The Supreme Court passed on technical claims of error, and "finding no error the verdicts are to stand." Judge Thayer knows this, but laymen may not. Yet Judge Thayer refers to the verdict as "approved by the Supreme Judicial Court."

No wonder that Judge Thayer's opinion has confirmed old doubts of the guilt of these two Italians and aroused new anxieties concerning the resources of our law to avoid grave miscarriage of justice. The courageous stand taken by the *Boston Herald* has enlisted the support of some of the most distinguished citizens of Massachusetts. President Comstock of Radcliffe College; Dr. Samuel M. Crothers; Mrs. Margaret Deland, the novelist; Professor W. E. Hocking, the philosopher; Mr. John F. Moors; Professor Samuel E. Morison, the historian; President Neilson of Smith College; Mr. Reginald H. Smith, author of *Justice and the Poor;* Dean Sperry of the Harvard Theological School; Professor Frank W. Taussig, the economist, are among those who have asked for a dispassionate hearing on all the facts. The *Independent* has thus epitomized this demand: —

Because of the increasing doubt that surrounds the question of the guilt of these men, springing from the intrinsic character of Judge Thayer's decision, and instanced by the judgment of the *Herald* editorial writer and other observers whose impartiality is unquestioned, we strongly hope that a new trial will be granted. It is important to note that the appeal is being made on the basis of new evidence never passed on before by the Supreme Court.[1]

[1] November 6, 1926, p. 514.

No narrow, merely technical, question is thus presented. The Supreme Judicial Court of Massachusetts will be called upon to search the whole record
in order to determine whether Judge Thayer duly
observed the traditional standards of fairness and
reason which govern the conduct of an Anglo-American
judge, particularly in a capital case. This Court has
given us the requirements by which Judge Thayer's
decision is to be measured and the tests which it will
use in determining whether a new trial shall be granted.

The various statements of the extent of the power and of
limitations upon the right to grant new trials * * * must
yield to the fundamental test, in aid of which most rules have
been formulated, that such motions ought not to be granted
unless on a survey of the whole case it appears to the judicial
conscience and judgment that otherwise a miscarriage of justice
will result.[1]

Nor must a new trial be withheld, where in justice
it is called for, because thereby encouragement will
be given to improper demands for a new trial. For,
as the Chief Justice of Massachusetts has announced,
courts cannot close "their eyes to injustice on account
of facility of abuse." [2]

With these legal canons as a guide, the outcome
ought not to be in doubt.

I have sought to give in perspective, and so far as
possible through the mouths of judge and witnesses,
the facts of a particular case which has attracted
world-wide attention, and not to call into question

[1] *Davis* v. *Boston Elevated Ry.*, 235 Mass. 482, 496.
[2] *Berggren* v. *Mutual Life Ins. Co.*, 231 Mass. 173, 177.

the Anglo-American system of criminal justice in general, or that of Massachusetts in particular. American criminal procedure has its defects. That we know on the authority of all who have made a special study of its working. But its essentials have behind them the vindication of centuries. Only ignorant and uncritical minds will find in an occasional striking illustration of its fallibilities an attack upon its foundations or lack of loyalty to its purposes. All systems of law, however wise, are administered through men, and therefore may occasionally disclose the frailties of men. Perfection may not be demanded of law, but the capacity to correct errors of inevitable frailty is the mark of a civilized legal mechanism. Grave injustices, as a matter of fact, do arise even under the most civilized systems of law and despite adherence to the forms of procedure intended to safeguard against them.

By way of illustration let us recall three striking instances in which the machinery of the criminal law worked injustice which was later corrected. The effectiveness of English criminal justice is properly held up to us for our imitation. Yet it was that system which, in a case turning on identification, sent Adolf Beck to prison for five years, although it was subsequently established that Beck was as innocent of the crime as the judge who sentenced him.[1] It was this grave miscarriage of justice which led, in 1907, to the establishment of the English Court of Criminal Appeal, with its very wide power of revision of criminal cases. In 1922 a

[1] Watson, Trial of Adolf Beck.

Chinese student named Wan was convicted of murder
in the courts of the city of Washington. The Court of
Appeals of the District of Columbia (ordinarily the final
court of appeal in such cases) affirmed the conviction.
Luckily the Supreme Court of the United States,
doubtless influenced by the intervention of Mr. John
W. Davis, exercised its prerogative of grace and allowed an appeal. The Court then unanimously found
both the trial court and the Court of Appeals in error,
reversed the conviction, and ordered a new trial because
of a singularly abhorrent resort by the police to "third
degree" methods in extorting confessions from the
Chinaman.[1] Wan was twice put on trial, twice thereafter the juries refused to convict, and the Government thereupon quashed the indictments; and Wan —
after seven years in jail under harrowing circumstances
— was given his liberty.[2] It should be noted that the
review exercised by the Supreme Court in this case is
seldom assumed by that Court. But for this unusual
intervention Wan would have been executed, despite all the formal observances of the criminal procedure of the District of Columbia; and high-minded
men and women, without opportunity or time to
exercise independent judgment on the case, would
have assumed that the trial court and the Court of
Appeals of the District of Columbia had served as
ample safeguards against an unwarranted hanging
carried out under the forms of law. Finally, last year
the Governor of New Jersey pardoned an Italian named

[1] *Wan v. United States,* 266 U. S. 1 (1924).
[2] See *New York Times,* June 17, 1926.

Morello convicted of murdering his wife because later investigation showed that a fatally wrong meaning was given to his testimony through misunderstandings of the interpreter.[1]   The efforts that were made to secure revision of judicial judgment in the Beck case, in the Wan case, and in the Morello case in no wise imply an attempt to undermine the necessary safeguards of society against crime in England, or in the District of Columbia, or in New Jersey.   Rather do they reveal confidence in our institutions and their capacity to rectify errors.   They also serve to warn against too marked an assumption that, because ordinarily the criminal machinery affords ample safeguards against perversions of justice, a situation may not arise where extraordinary circumstances have deflected the operation of the normal procedure.

[1] See *New York Times*, May 20, 21, 23, and June 5, 1926.

APPENDIX A

COUNSEL for Sacco and Vanzetti have subjected the relative weight of the Morelli-Madeiros and Sacco-Vanzetti hypotheses as an explanation of the South Braintree crime to the following tabular study.[1]

CHARACTER OF ACCUSED

Medeiros-Morelli

Typical gangsters and gunmen of the worst type.

Sacco-Vanzetti

One of them an industrious workman with a family and a savings bank deposit, and no previous criminal record. The other a fish peddler never before his arrest accused of crime. Both unpopular as pacifists and extreme radicals.

MOTIVE

Desperate need of funds for lawyer and bail before trial for serious Federal offence. Source of income through robbing freight cars blocked by U. S. Marshal and R.R. police.

Robbery for private gain alleged. No claim or evidence that either defendant ever received or had any part of the stolen money.

[1] Brief of William G. Thompson and Herbert B. Ehrmann on behalf of defendants in *Commonwealth* v. *Sacco and Vanzetti*, January Sitting, 1927, No. 5583.

OPPORTUNITY TO PLAN CRIME

Had been repeatedly stealing large shipments from *Slater and Morrill* and *Rice and Hutchins* of *South Braintree* after a member of the gang had "spotted" them in that place.

None alleged.

ACCUSATION BY CONFEDERATE

Direct testimony of participant.

None.

IDENTIFICATION BY OTHERS

Opportunity restricted, but Joe, Mancini, and Benkosky identified from photographs by Government as well as defence witnesses. No available photographs of Mike or Frank. Undoubted resemblance of Joe Morelli to Sacco in many particulars.

Some identification of Sacco; very slight of Vanzetti at the scene of the murder. Identifications open not only to doubt, but to the gravest suspicion owing to unprecedented manner of displaying these defendants, previous identifications of other criminals by same witnesses, changes in stories, suppression of testimony, manifestly impossible details such as the man identified as Vanzetti using "clear and unmistakable English," and the man identified as Sacco having an unusually large hand.

ALIBI

Full of contradictions as to Morellis. None by Medeiros.

Testified to by many reputable witnesses.

Consciousness of Guilt

Alleged motion to draw gun on officer, uncontradicted.

Falsehoods consistent with nothing but consciousness of guilt of crime charged. Confession by Medeiros.

Alleged motion to draw gun on officer — contradicted.

Falsehoods explained by terror felt by radicals and draft evaders at time of persecution of "reds" two days after murder or suicide of a friend while in the custody of Department of Justice officials.

Bullets

One fired from pistol of type owned by Joe Morelli (Colt 32), and five from type owned by Mancini ("Star" or "Steyr," 765 mm.).

One only claimed to have been fired by weapon of Sacco, ' and none by Vanzetti. Sharp disagreement of experts, but if real opinion of one of the Government's experts had been known at the time of the trial he would have proved a *defence witness*.

Other Corroborative Matter

Morellis were American-born and could have used "clear and unmistakable" English. *Every member of the murder party accounted for*. Unwillingness of Morelli lawyer to state anything tending to implicate his former clients in the South Braintree murders.

Testimony shows that cap claimed to be Sacco's was *not* identified by Kelly, and effort to connect Vanzetti's popular make of revolver with Berardelli's supported by most remote type of evidence, including confused records of gun-shop offered by an ex-agent (unrevealed) of the Department of Justice. Does not account for other members of the party.

Stolen Money

Medeiros' possession of $2,800 immediately thereafter (about his "split" of the total sum stolen).

None. On the contrary, when arrested, Sacco and Vanzetti, supposed to be in possession of over $15,000, and ex-hypothesis, to be accomplished automobile thieves, were using street cars after an unsuccessful attempt to borrow a friend's six-year-old Overland.

Attitude of Authorities

Seriously offer statements and affidavits of Morellis denying participation in crime. Declined request of defendant's counsel to interview *all witnesses* jointly to avoid vulgar contest of affidavits. Declined to investigate.

Anti-Red excitement capitalized; highly prejudicial cross-examination as to draft evasion and anarchistic opinions and associations; patriotic speeches and charge by Judge to jury; interference by Department of Justice agents who believed defendants innocent; suppression of testimony favorable to defence; intentionally misleading testimony of expert on vital point.

APPENDIX B

THE following editorial appeared in the *Boston Herald*, Tuesday, October 26, 1926.

WE SUBMIT—

In our opinion Nicola Sacco and Bartolomeo Vanzetti ought not to be executed on the warrant of the verdict returned by a jury on July 14, 1921. We do not know whether these men are guilty or not. We have no sympathy with the half-baked views which they profess. But as months have merged into years and the great debate over this case has continued, our doubts have solidified slowly into convictions, and reluctantly we have found ourselves compelled to reverse our original judgment. We hope the supreme judicial court will grant a new trial on the basis of the new evidence not yet examined in open court. We hope the Governor will grant another reprieve to Celestino Madeiros so that his confession may be canvassed in open court. We hope, in case our supreme bench finds itself unable legally to authorize a new trial, that our Governor will call to his aid a commission of disinterested men of the highest intelligence and character to make an independent investigation in his behalf, and that the Governor himself at first hand will participate in that examination, if, as a last resort, it shall be undertaken.

We have read the full decision in which Judge Webster Thayer, who presided at the original trial, renders his decision against the application for a new trial, and we submit that it carries the tone of the advocate rather than the arbitrator. At the outset he refers to "the verdict of a jury approved by the supreme court of this commonwealth" and later he repeats that sentence. We respectfully submit that the supreme court never approved that verdict. What the court did is stated in its own words thus: "We have examined carefully all the exceptions in so far as argued, and finding no error the verdicts are to stand." The supreme court did not vindicate the verdict. The court certified that, whether the verdict was right or wrong, the trial judge performed his duty under the law in a legal manner. The supreme court overruled a bill of exceptions but expressed no judgment whatever as to the validity of the verdict or the guilt of the defendants. Judge Thayer knows this, yet allows himself to refer to the verdict as "approved by the supreme court."

We submit, also, that Judge Thayer's language contains many innuendos which surely are unfortunate in such a document. The petition for a new trial is based in part on the affidavits of two men, Letherman and Weyand, connected respectively with the United States government for thirty-six years and eight years, and both now holding responsible positions out of the federal service. Judge Thayer says that one of these men "seems, for some reason, to be willing to go the limit in his affidavits against the government of the United States," and he refers to "prejudiced affidavits, which appear to be quite easily obtained nowadays." The changes are rung on certain phrases, also, as "fraudulent conspiracy between these two great governments," meaning the governments of the United States and Massachusetts. The judge asserts a conspiracy charge which was not made by counsel for the defense; he asks "who pumped this curiosity into Madeiros"; he compliments the prosecution and refers slightingly to counsel for the defense.

We submit that evidence, if any, in the files of the department of justice having any bearing on this case ought to be examined in open court, or examined in private by the United States attorney-general and reported upon by him before this case shall finally be decided. We have no idea what the files may contain. Mr. Weyand said in his affidavit: "The conviction was the result of co-operation between the Boston agents of the department of justice and the district attorney." We do not know that this is true, but we know there was co-operation; the department and the attorney joined in placing a spy in the cell next to Sacco's, and the prosecution admitted the fact in court.

Now as to Madeiros: A criminal with a bad record, true, and under sentence of death. But the government relied in part on one of his confessions to convict him of a murder. His evidence was accepted against himself when his own life was at stake. His evidence now is offered in behalf of two other men whose lives also are at stake. We submit that Madeiros should be placed on the stand in open court, facing a jury and a judge, and subjected to examination and cross-examination. He may be lying, but the criterion here is not what a judge may think about it but what a jury might think about it. The question is — Would the new evidence be a real factor with a jury in reaching a decision?

We submit that doubt is cast on the verdict of the jury by the important affidavit made after the trial by Capt. C. H. Proctor of the state police. On the stand, testifying as an expert, his evidence was understood by the jury and the judge to be that the fatal bullet issued from Sacco's pistol. Careful examination of the record discloses curious facts. Capt. Proctor did not here reply to direct questions. His affidavit states what the record implies, that a device was fixed up in advance for dodging direct answer to a direct question. His replies were understood to mean that he believed the bullet came from that weapon. He allowed that impression to go abroad. But his affidavit contradicts that testimony. Now when the supreme court dealt with that point it expressed no opinion as to whether or not an "ambiguous answer" had been arranged to "obtain a conviction." The court ruled only that the trial judge had decided that no such pre-arrangement had been made, and that the supreme court could not "as matter of law" set aside the ruling of the trial judge.

For these and other reasons we hope that the resources of our laws will prove adequate to obtain a new trial. Let it be remembered that the new trial is asked for on the basis of evidence never before the supreme court previously. The court has ruled on exceptions to the old trial, never on all evidence for a new one. If on a new trial the defendants shall again be found guilty we shall be infinitely better off than if we proceed to execution on the basis of the trial already held; the shadow of doubt, which abides in the minds of large numbers of patient investigators of this whole case, will have been removed. And if on second trial Sacco and Vanzetti should be declared guilt-less, everybody would rejoice that no monstrous injustice shall have been done. We submit these views with no reference whatever to the personality of the defendants, and without allusion now to that atmosphere of radicalism of which we heard so much in 1921.

A SELECTED LIST OF TITLES IN THE
Universal Library

History and Political Science

Literature, Criticism, Drama, and Poetry

Psychology

Titles of General Interest